Learning New Techniques with Microsoft Word 2010

Doug Hewitt & Robin Hewitt

Champion Writers

Atlanta – Beijing – Harbin – Washington

Learning New Techniques with Microsoft Word 2010
First Edition
Copyright © 2009 by Doug Hewitt & Robin Hewitt

International Standard Book Number:
ISBN-13: 978-1-60830-021-1
ISBN-10: 1-60830-021-8

Printed in the United States of America.

Disclaimer
The author of this book is not affiliated with any software maker and/or its affiliates. Therefore, the views and opinions expressed in this book do not represent the views and opinions of any software maker and/or its affiliates.

The information presented in this book is for reference only. The author(s) and publisher strive to provide accurate information. Several factors will create different user experiences than the one presented in this book. These factors include variations of software versions, patches, operating systems, configurations, and customizations. This book is not warranted to be error-free or up-to-date.

Reference resources listed in this book, such as website addresses, may have changed after this book was published.

The author(s) and the publisher shall have neither liability nor responsibility to any person or entity with respect to any loss or damages arising from the information contained in this publication.

This book was written with perseverance and an eye toward the future. We dedicate this book to our grandchildren with the hope that they can realize the benefits of these attributes. Our list of grandchildren is expected to lengthen, but as it currently stands, it includes Tarissa, Gavin, Genna, Kenna, Gabby, Jake, Kylin, and Bryan. May they live long and prosper!

About the Author

Doug and Robin Hewitt are a husband-and-wife writing team living in Mayodan, North Carolina. They also do college consulting and give speaking engagements on their methods of ensuring college success. Their books are filled with strategies to win scholarships and to use Microsoft Word to write top-notch essays. Their book about college funding, the Free College Resource Book: Inside Secrets From Two Parents Who Put Five Kids Through College for Next to Nothing, helps students find free funding for college with scholarships and grants. They are currently writing a follow-up to Learning New Techniques with Microsoft Word 2010 with a Microsoft Excel 2010 book.

We Love to Hear from You!

Every reader of this book has something to say that we may learn from. Your opinions and comments are invaluable to us. While every precaution has been taken in the preparation of this book, there remains the possibility that errors or omissions still exist. If you find errors or omissions in this book, please check out the publisher's website and review all documented errata. If you do not find your issue on that list, please submit your comments to us, and we will update our website and correct all of the known issues in the next release.

Please note that the author(s) is unable to help you with any technical issues related to the topics included in this book. Due to the volume of messages we receive from our readers, we are unable to respond to every message; however, please be assured that your message will be carefully read, considered, and provided with a response when warranted.

When contacting us, please visit publisher's website at:

http://www.championwriters.com

Contents at a Glance

Table of Contents

Conventions Used in This Book

The following conventions are used in this book:

Italic is used for:
- Program Names, pathnames, and filenames
- Web addresses (URLs)
- Book or article titles

Constant Width is used for:
- Source code examples
- SQL statements

Bold is used for
- Emphasis
- Menu item or command

Please pay attention to the following icons:

 Warning: this message should be carefully reviewed to prevent issues or problems.

 Tips: This message provides you some shortcuts or efficient ways to solve problems.

 Real World: Real world working experience summary for the related topic.

 Notes: important information to remember.

 Security: features that related to application security.

 Resources: online or offline resources.

 Tools: special tools for application development, integration, or testing.

Chapter 1

■ ■ ■

Let's Go Backstage

Why We're Here

The title says it all.

We're here to teach you new techniques using Microsoft Word 2010.

This book is designed for casual Word users, beginners, and for people who are using Word 2010 for the first time. If you've used Word before, you might see little outward changes at first. This is the case if you're upgrading from Word 2007. If, however, you're jumping to Word 2010 from an earlier version of Word, you might be baffled at first by the new way that Word 2010 presents command choices to the user.

Word 2010, like the 2007 incarnation, uses the Ribbon as the main interface.

Figure 1-1. *The Ribbon under the Home Tab*

You might notice the most obvious change is the look of the **Office Button**. Instead of the large round button in the upper left corner of the interface, beside the *Home* tab, Word 2010 has a square tab-like button.

The **Office Button** is one of the changes in Word 2010, not only in appearance, but what it prompts Word to do when selected.

   The **Office Button** in Word 2007

 The **Office Button** in Word 2010

But we'll save our talk about the **Office Button** for later. After all, this is just the Introduction. In the meantime, what are the other objectives of this book? If you're new to using Word, every technique will be new to you. To that end, we're going to present some simple Word projects in creating documents. We believe the best way of learning is doing. We encourage you to follow along with our projects on a computer. That way, the techniques we present will sink into the cranial matter better. Speaking of cranial matter, we hope to present an instructional book that is also entertaining to read, not stuffy like some other (unmentioned) books.

By the way, if you've looked through the shelves at your local bookstore for books that help people learn and use Microsoft Word, you might have been discouraged by the number of pages in some of these books. Hundreds and hundreds of pages of detailed instruction greet you. For some books, the page count approaches 1,000!

So we're going to try to help people learn Word 2010 basics and techniques that will help with simple projects like putting together a family newsletter. Or maybe composing a letter to a loved one. We will also consider college students who need to learn how to use Microsoft Word 2010 in order to write term papers and the letter home to ask for a few extra dollars. We'll get you started, show you the basics, and then leave it to you to use Word Help to delve into any intricacies that interest you.

We wanted to write a book for beginners and for users who want to know about the new features of Word 2010. We wanted to write a book that doesn't intimidate readers with small text and thousands of topics. We come at this as writers and readers, not computer programmers, and so we can appreciate good wording.

A Sneak Peek

As we already mentioned, we'll be putting in screenshots of what you'll be looking at with your Word 2010 screen. With that in mind, we'll jump ahead and give you a sneak peak at the first screenshot. When you open Microsoft Word 2010, you'll see a screen that already has a new document opened. In a way, you're already in gear and can start typing text.

But how do you save your document?

You do it with the new Word stage, the *Backstage* view. It appears when you select the **Office Button**.

 When we tell you to select a tab or command, this is performed by moving the selection arrow over the tab or command and left clicking the mouse button.

Let's start at the beginning, though, and show you how to open Word 2010. The steps to open Word 2010 depend on the type of operating system you have. Most personal computers run on a Microsoft operating system (OS, pronounced *Oh Ess*, is how tech-savvy people refer to it), and we'll describe the steps for the Microsoft OS. If you have something else, check with your computer's documentation.

To open Word 2010:

1) Move your mouse to point the cursor at the **Start** button, usually in the lower left corner on your computer monitor.
2) Press the left mouse button with the pointer over the **Start** button to select it.
3) Left click on **All Programs**.
4) Use the scroll bar to scroll through the programs until you find the *Microsoft Office* folder.
5) Left click on the *Microsoft Office* folder.
6) Left click on **Microsoft Word 2010**.

Now, wasn't that easy? You're on your way to learning new techniques with Word 2010. Now, select the **Office Button** and Word 2010 takes you to the *Backstage* view.

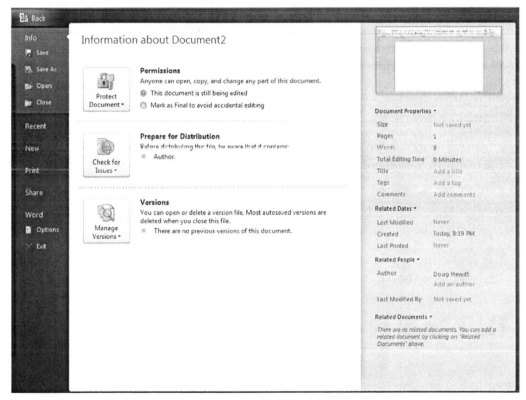

Figure 1-2. *The Backstage View*

As you can see, you're presented with a series of command options. We'll go through some of those commands in the next chapter. For now, congratulations. You're on your way to using Microsoft Word 2010.

Introducing Backstage View

Imagine you're at a play, watching the acting performances on a stage. It's a wonderful play, a musical, and the performances are flawless. But a lot of work goes on behind the curtain. Between acts, staging is moved, costumes changes, lighting altered. And before the play begins, the entire stage needs to be set.

These are things that are done with the Backstage view in Word 2010.

In this chapter, we'll walk through many of the screens that show up in Backstage view. We'll talk about a few techniques that you can use to get the full use out of its features.

The Backstage view is a new screen in Microsoft Word, but we think you'll find many of the features are familiar to commands in previous versions.

New Document

Let's open a new document. Documents are opened from the Backstage view. That way, you can address properties of the document before you begin work.

1) Click on the **Office Button**.
2) The Backstage view appears.
3) Click on **New**.

A screen appears with available commands for you to choose what kind of new document you're planning on creating.

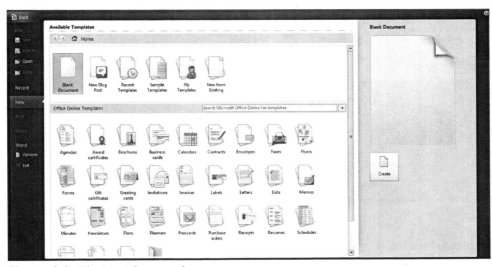

Figure 1-3. *The New Commands*

There are a number of templates you can choose from existing in Word 2010. Or, if you don't see what you need, you can check for Office Online Templates (if you're online). For most situations, templates in the Sample Templates location will suit the need.

But we encourage you to look around at the different templates available. We're not going to list them all here. That's not the purpose of this book. We're here to teach you techniques.

We would like to point out the option *New from Existing*. If you have a document such as a class essay that you'd like to use as a template, you can choose this option. It will keep your headers and other document information. Afterward, it will appear in the Recent Templates location. This is also a great option for reports, letters, journal entries, and recipes. Use your imagination!

Document Information

We've double-clicked on the **Blank document** command.

Because we have previously opened a document, Word 2010 assigns the number "2" to our new document, and so that's why it's given the name "*Document2*" until we give it a name later. After opening your new document, click on the **Office Button** again.

Choose **Info** if not already selected. A screen appears with information about the current document, *Document2* in our situation.

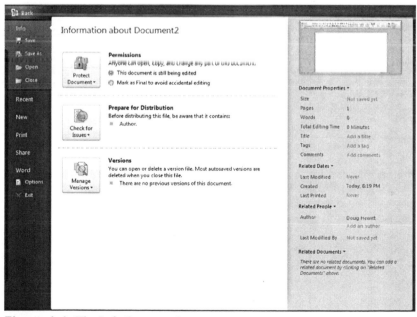

Figure 1-4. *The Info Commands*

There are 3 main categories in the Info category.

- Permissions
- Prepare for Distribution
- Versions

Let's look at each of these in turn.

Permissions

Click on the **Permissions** option.

As you can see from the previous screenshot, our document was still being edited and anyone can open, change (including delete!) any part, and copy the document. Do you care? If you're writing a document used in business, you might not want everyone to see it.

What about if you're working in payroll and your document will list executive salaries? Or perhaps it's a journal entry detailing your secret love life. Maybe permissions are a good idea.

Also, there are some institutional requirements to consider. For example, if the document details work procedures, an auditor of work practices might ask to see the document. The auditor might ask how you know it hasn't been changed by someone else. If you don't have permissions set, you won't have an answer to please to auditor.

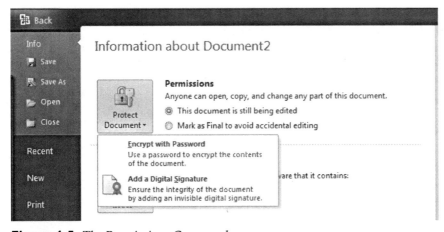

Figure 1-5. *The Permissions Commands*

You have the option here of setting a password or a digital signature. A digital signature is like an actual John Henry in the digital age. It's your signature, a mark that identifies you as a person. This can help to deter forgery documents.

 If you save your document as a *Word97 - 2003 Document*, you'll also have a Compatibility Mode option in the Info section of the Backstage view. This gives you information about formatting in different versions of Word.

Prepare for Distribution

There are some things you can do to prepare your document for distribution. Also, this category can let you know some of the issues that might pertain to your document in particular, in the format in which it is saved, for example.

Here are some of the issues pertaining to this chapter that Word 2010 tells us about as we write.

Prepare for Distribution

Before distributing this file, be aware that it contains:

- Document properties, author, related people and related dates.
- Custom XML data.
- Headers.
- Content that cannot be checked for accessibility issues because of the current file type

Information about our chapter that might be of interest to people with different versions of Word.

In this category, you can also check for issues.

1) Click on the **Check for Issues** command.
2) A dialog box appears.

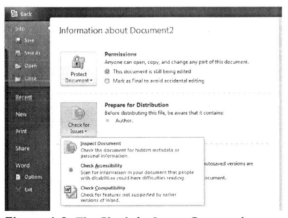

Figure 1-6. *The Check for Issues Commands*

Note that you can:

- Inspect the document for hidden metadata or personal information.
- Scan the document information that people with disabilities could have trouble reading.
- Check for features not supported by earlier versions of Word.

 If you're not sure who will be reading your document, it might be a good idea to have a document compatible with earlier versions of Word. Usually, earlier versions can be read by later versions. This may not be true vice versa.

Versions

Click on the **Versions** command.

Note that if this is a new document and you've just started using Word 2010, you'll not have very many (if any at all) versions of the document you're working with.

But with this command, you might find a useful new technique for working with a document. Have you ever wished you could move back in time to 10, 15, or maybe even 45 minutes to when you were working on a document and made a particular decision on how to present your data and made a decision that didn't work out?

Okay, maybe you're one of those Word wonders who saves multiple copies of the same document with slight title variation as you write, but you would be one of the few and far between.

Word 2010 has an auto-save feature that allows you to move back in time to a version of the document that precedes that ill-fated formatting decision.

Here's what you'll see initially with the Versions command.

Figure 1-7. *The Versions Commands*

Note that you have three options to choose from here.

- Compare your document version with the one you most recently saved.
- Recover a draft version of your document.
- Delete all of your draft versions.

We'll give you a snapshot of some of the options we have as we write this chapter.

Versions

You can open or delete a version file. Most autosaved versions are
deleted when you close this file.

- Monday 10/12/2009 10:06 PM (autosave)

- Monday 10/12/2009 9:55 PM (autosave)

- Monday 10/12/2009 9:45 PM (autosave)

- Monday 10/12/2009 9:34 PM (autosave)

- Monday 10/12/2009 9:23 PM (autosave)

Move back in time to look at autosaved
versions of the document you're working with.

You might not want to clutter up your Backstage view with loads of autosaved versions of your
document, but they're out of the way …, *offstage*, so you should consider keeping them in case you
need them someday.

Save As

Click on **Save As** to save your document.

When you choose this command, you are presented with options of where to save your document and
what name to give it. You also have other options from this dialog box.
Note the **Tools** command button at the bottom of the dialog box. Click on the button.

Figure 1-8. *The Tools Commands*

The Tools command button allows you **Map a Network Drive** (for people on a network), choose your **Save Options**, choose **General Options** for the document, select **Web Options**, and **Compress Pictures**.

 Compressing pictures allows you to make your file smaller.

Save Options gives you two useful options that could be time-savers down the road. Select **Save Options** and note you can select the default format of your documents when you save them. If you're constantly saving as Word97-2003 Documents, you can select it as the default file format here.

Also with **Save Options**, you can select how often you want the autosave feature to save a version of your document. You get to choose the increments in time you can move back in!

Document Properties Pane

Over to the right side of the screen, you'll see the Document Properties Pane. You can view information here about your document and enter information, too.

One handy feature is the list of editing time on the document. You may think you've been working for hours and find that you've only had the document open for forty-five minutes!

Other useful information tidbits include:

- When the document was last printed.
- When the document was last modified.
- How many words the document has.
- The file size of the document.

Figure 1-9. *The Document Properties Pane*

Note that you can also type comments here. For home users, you could type the reason why you started your journal document, for example, or how many pages you hope the final document turns out to be, or what the purpose of the document is.

Tags are useful to enter here for documents that will be published on the web. These tags can help generate hits. Your list of **Related Documents** can be useful, for example, if you're putting together a catalog of different documents.

1)   Click on **Related Documents**.

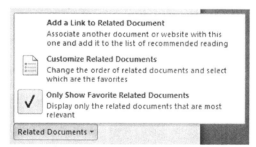

Figure 1-10. *The Related Documents Commands*

As you can see, you can:

- Link to a related document or website.
- Change the order of the related documents and mark some as favorites.
- Select to show only favorite related documents.

Share

Going back to the list of commands on the left of your screen, let's look at the Share commands.

1) Click on **Share**.

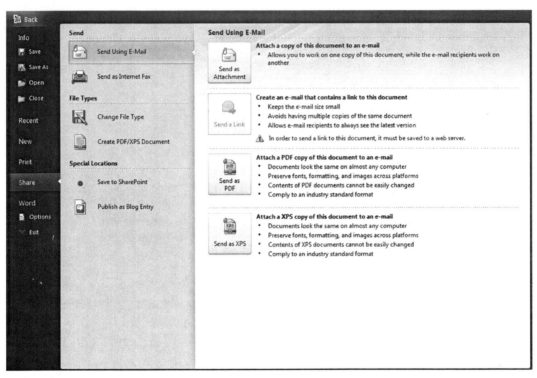

Figure 1-11. *The Share Commands*

You have two Send options.

- Send via email
- Send as Internet Fax.

There are two file type options.

- Change the file type of your document.
- Create a PDF/XPS document.

There are two Special Location options.

- Save to Sharepoint.
- Publish as a blog entry.

Many companies use Sharepoint to share information. The ability of employees to upload their work to Sharepoint sites with the click of a mouse is a great new technique of Word 2010.

Word

On the bottom of the left bar of commands, you'll see the *Word* group. Click on **Word** to bring up a menu of commands. One of the commands on this list is **Options**, which is also in the *Word* group. It's just a couple of separate paths to arrive at the same menu, **Word Options**.

Figure 1-12. *The Word Tools Commands*

These commands offer you ways to contact Microsoft if you need help or to offer suggestions. The self-support command allows you to the online support site, and Microsoft Office Online has product updates, clip art, templates you can download, and other useful features.

You can also check for product updates, customize Office, launch the System Information Tool, and of course go to the Options menu of commands.

Word Options

Word Options is where you can set up the way you work with Word 2010. Click on Word Options, and you're presented with the General option settings.

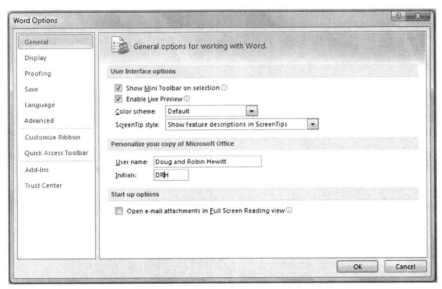

Figure 1-13. *The Word Options Commands*

We'll cover the Mini-Toolbar later, but if you don't want it popping up every time you select text, here's the checkbox to disable it. Live preview is another great feature that shows you what your selection is going to look like as you hover your pointer over various choices. For example, you could select text, the roll your pointer over different font sizes. The text will change depending on the size under your pointer. It's a preview!

See the small "i" with a small circle around it at the end of the first two checkbox commands? Hover your pointer over the information circle to get a popup description box of the command. *The list of Word Options command menus.*

- General
- Display
- Proofing
- Save
- Language
- Advanced
- Customize Ribbon
- Quick Access Toolbar
- Add-Ins
- Trust Center

We're not going to go over each of the command menus in the left pane at this point of the book. Remember how there were two paths to the Options list? The same is true for some, if not all, of the other menus. We'll get to some of them as we work through examples and techniques in this book. We suggest you peruse through the settings and see which options suit your method of working.

 Use **Word Help** (the little blue question mark near the upper right corner). Type in menu commands to see what they do.

But we do want to cover a couple of the menu choices at this point because we think they are important and can fundamentally change the way you use Word.

Customize Ribbon

The Ribbon is the bar across the top of the document that has groups of commands. We'll talk more about the Ribbon later. But for now, click on **Customize Ribbon**. You'll see that you can choose commands from the list on the left and move them to Ribbon group choices on the right. This is a great way to set up your Ribbon with the commands that you use most or that make the most sense to you.

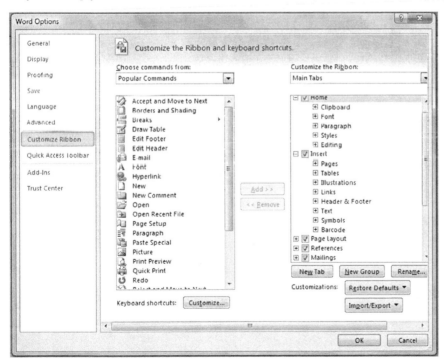

Figure 1-14. *The Customize Ribbon Commands*

You might find yourself using the same ten commands over and over. But, they are under different Ribbon tabs. You can arrange all of your most-used Ribbon commands together in the same group. Arrange them in the order you use them, if that suits you.

You'll find this can be a big time-saver in the long run, although it will take you a few minutes to set up your commands and a few sessions of working with Word to get used to them.

Quick Access Toolbar

The other list of menus commands we wanted to look at here is the *Quick Access Toolbar*.

> 1) From the *Word Options* menu, click on **Quick Access Toolbar**.

The Customize the Quick Access Toolbar pane opens.

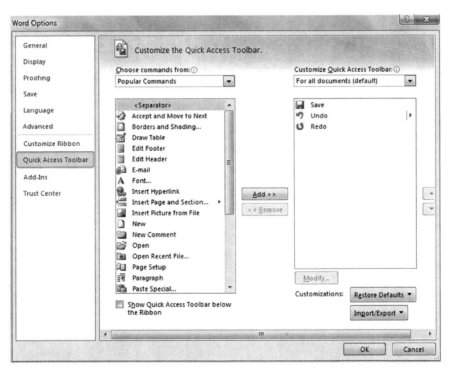

Figure 1-15. *The Quick Access Toolbar Commands*

The process is the same here. Move the commands you use most from the left column to the right column.

> 1) Highlight the command on the left.
> 2) Click on **Add >>**.

We'll show you the location of the Quick Access Toolbar later. But this is another place where you can place your most-used commands. The quality about the Quick Access Toolbar that sets it apart is that it is present no matter which Ribbon tab you select.

Summary

We've shown you around the Backstage view in Microsoft Word 2010. It's a place from which you can set up the shining document that will be presented to the world (or coworkers, or the teacher, or a friend, or ..., well, you get the idea) by doing the backstage work necessary to make the play production shine.

We've shown you where you can customize your Quick Access Toolbar and Ribbon commands. As you work through this book, keep these options in mind. You may find yourself wishing for a command icon in a particular Ribbon tab.

Document properties were discussed in this chapter, and they are also set in the Backstage view. We've also shown you some new techniques, such as saving your document to a Sharepoint site. Now that the backstage work has been done, we can move on to the main production!

Chapter 2

■ ■ ■

Working with Text

Introduction

Now that we've shown you how to create documents and save them on your computer via the Backstage view, we'll get started on working with text in this chapter.

For Word users who are familiar with Word 2007, some of the instructions might be rehashing commands that you're already familiar with. For example, you might already know how to add more spacing between the lines of your text. Or to have a sentence or maybe just one word in **bold** or *italics*. Word 2010 is a powerful word processing application, and we could devote an entire book on working with text. But that's not what we're here for. We're here to show you the basics and some new techniques. Once you're comfortable with working with the basics, and you get comfortable using the basic Word 2010 *Tabs* and **Commands**, you can explore all of the intricacies of each command available in in the Ribbon If you have the inclination.

We're going to open a new document and look at the *Home* tab and groups and other items you'll be looking at. In effect, we're going from the back stage to center stage, where we'll be ready to begin our work.

So let's get on with some simple lessons on working with text.

New Document

Open a new document, a blank document, and you'll be looking at the *Home* Ribbon. You'll see a line of tabs above the Ribbon, and the *Home* tab will be the first one, just to the right of the **Office Button**.

1) To bring along the newcomers to Word:
2) Click on the **Office Button**.
3) Click on **New**.
4) Double click on **Blank Document**.

Your new document will open. Say hello to the *Home* Ribbon.

Figure 2-1. *The Home Ribbon*

There's a lot of information here. If you're new to Word, it might seem like there's too much visual information here. Where does someone start?

Let's start by looking at how information and commands are organized. Once you see how commands are grouped (*hint, hint*), you'll be more at ease. We'll also keep reminding you about Microsoft Help. In the upper right corner of the screen, there's a question mark with a blue circle around. If you need help or have questions, click on Microsoft Help.

From there, type in the subject matter of your question. This is not *Jeopardy!*, so just type in a few key words. It doesn't have to be in the form of a question.

Now, let's look at what you see when you open a new document.

Home Ribbon Screen Features

Let's look at the main features of your Word user interface. That's what it is, the interface between Word and you. It's the mechanism, the means, by which you interact with the Word document. It displays information for you to read and presents commands for you to give.

Tabs	Below the document name is a row of words. These are called the *Tabs*. Left clicking on a tab gives you a choice of commands related to that tab. The tabs you'll see here are: **Home**, **Insert**, **Page Layout**, **References**, **Mailings**, **Review**, and **View**.
Ribbon	The *Ribbon* is a row directly below the tabs. In the *Ribbon*, functions and commands are displayed such as **Paste** and **Format Painter**. These commands are grouped together in *Groups*.
Group	Each group of commands is named at the bottom of the *Group*. The *Groups* you'll see on your opening screen are *Clipboard, Font, Paragraph, Styles*, and *Editing*. Each *Group* is separated by a border of a slightly different shade of color.
Launcher	Most, but not all, *Groups* have a small square button at the bottom right of each *group's* border. This is called the *Launcher*. Left clicking the *Launcher* will open a dialog box with more related commands.
Help	At the far right side of the row of *Tabs* is a small circle with a question mark in it. Left clicking this will launch *Word Help*.
Quick Access Toolbar	Above the row of tabs, near the Office Button, are a couple of icons for **Save, Undo,** and **Redo**. This area is the Quick Access Toolbar. You can add commands that you frequently use to this area.

Office Button

The **Office Button** is to the left of the *Home* tab. It takes you to the Backstage view.

 Have a notebook open and pen at the ready when you work with Word and documents. Take notes on commands you think you'll use later. Write down the name of your file names with a brief description of the contents. A descriptive file name helps!

Let's take a closer look at each of the groups on the *Home* Ribbon. We'll save the *Clipboard* group for later. For now, think of the clipboard as a place where items are stored when you copy them for later pasting.

Fonts

A font is a typeface. It's how the letters look, the shape of them. Word 2010 has numerous fonts that you can work with. Let's take a look and see what kind of fonts you might want to try.

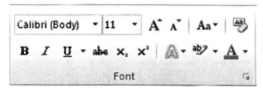 This is the *Font* group. It's under the *Home* tab. You can select commands in this group to change the appearance of your words.

For our version of Microsoft Word 2010, you can see that we have selected *Calibri* as the default font. Here's some sample text we've typed in for illustrative purposes.

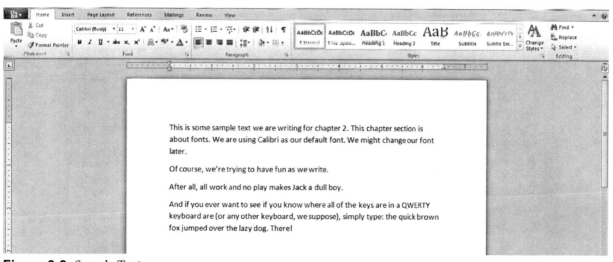

Figure 2-2. *Sample Text*

We would like to point out a couple of other features. You'll notice just below the Ribbon is a ruler.

This is the horizontal ruler. The vertical ruler is on the left side of the screen.

Also, in the *Styles* group, the **Normal** style is selected. This is the default style.

But, let's get back to our *Font* group.

 If you're sending your file to someone with another word processing application, they might not have some of the more exotic fonts. *Times New Roman* and *Ariel* are safe bets to use in your documents.

We're going to change the font and the font size of some of our text. If you're familiar with selecting text, be patient. We're writing this book so that it is of value to readers of all levels of Word competence.

To select text:

1) Move your pointer arrow over the text. It will become an I-beam cursor (vertical line with half-curls at the top and bottom).
2) Move the I-beam cursor to the front of the first letter of the first word of the text you want to select.
3) Press the left mouse button and keep it pressed.
4) Use the mouse to move the I-beam to just behind the last letter or character (such as the period of a sentence) of the text you want to select.
5) Release the left mouse button.

There is another way to select text if you're going to select an entire line or paragraph of text. You can also select multiple paragraphs.

To select a line or paragraph or multiple paragraphs:

1) Move your pointer arrow to the left of the text, making sure it is a pointer and not an I-beam. Align the point of the arrow with the first line of text you want to select.
2) Press the left mouse button and keep it pressed.
3) Use the mouse to move the pointer up or down. Entire lines of text will become highlighted as you move your pointer.
4) When all of the lines of text you want are selected, release the left mouse button.

 If you make a mistake and select the wrong text, simply click the mouse pointer (as an I-beam) anywhere in the document, and your text will be de-selected.

Now that you have the text selected, move your mouse pointer to the Font group. Use the font drop-down dialog box to select a different font. When you select a different font, the highlighted text will change to the font you've selected.

We've selected a new font for us, *Lucida Handwriting*.

some *sample text we are writing* for
ı is about fonts. We are using Calibri as our def:

Here's some text we selected and changed the font, which is a *Lucida Handwriting* font.

Okay, one last point on selecting text.

Click anywhere in your document when your pointer is an I-beam.

Press down the **cntl** key on the keyboard, otherwise known as the control key. While you have the **cntl** key pressed, briefly press the **A** key. Release both keys at the same time. Pressing these 2 keys at the same time selects all of the text in your document.

- **Cntl** + **A** = *select all text in the document.*

This is what's known as a *keyboard shortcut*. We won't be covering many in the book, but there are many. If they save you time, click on Word Help and type in "keyboard shortcuts." Word will give you a list of them. But don't worry. We'll show you the ones that we think are most important and most likely to save you time.

 Use a 3 x 5 index card to write down keyboard shortcuts for easy reference later.

Mini Toolbar

You might have noticed a useful feature in Word 2010. It's called a Mini Toolbar. It pops up when you select text. It's a convenient way to change text properties such as the font and selecting **bold** or *italics*. In our previous example with sample text, we went to the *Font* group with our mouse pointer and made our changes via the group commands.

Instead, you can use the Mini Toolbar commands.

The Mini Toolbar is a time-saving feature of Word 2010. It appears whenever you select text and has the most-used commands from the *Font* group.

We've selected some text in our sample text. See how the Mini Toolbar pops up? You may have to position your cursor above the text. Move your cursor around the selected text until the Mini Toolbar appears.

It is useful to think about the Mini Toolbar as a palette of commands at your fingertips when you select text. While the Ribbons that appear under the various Tabs gives you a complete milieu of colors and commands from which to work, the Mini Toolbar gives you the basic colors you need to paint a picture. and the commands on the Mini Toolbar are still there, in the Ribbon.

Note that these commands are mostly in the *Font* group, although the **Format Painter** (paintbrush) in the *Clipboard* group and **Increase Indent** and **Decrease Indent** are in the *Paragraph* group. Let's take a look at the Mini Toolbar.

Calibri as our default font. We might change

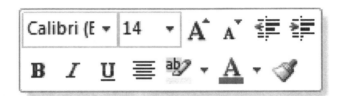

is we write.

Jack a dull boy.

iow where all of the keys are in a QWERTY

Figure 2-3. *The Mini Toolbar*

In Figure 2-3, you can see some of our text has been highlighted, indicated by a background color. Because we've selected text, namely, "dull boy," the Mini Toolbar has popped up on our screen.

We're going to go over the commands in the *Font* group, though. Just be aware that these commands are also available in the Mini Toolbar. Use the Mini Toolbar buttons or the buttons in the *Font* group, whichever method you're most comfortable with.

Turning the Mini Tool Bar On and Off

Before we get into the Font commands, and because we're focused on the Mini Toolbar, we're going to show you how to turn the Mini Toolbar on and off. To do this, we have to delve into the world of Word options. You can change all kinds of options in Word 2010, from having your documents automatically spell-checked to changing the Command buttons on the Ribbon.

To turn the Mini Toolbar off (or on):

1) Click on the **Office Button**.
2) Click on the **Options** button. It's near the bottom of the Backstage view pane on the left side of the screen.

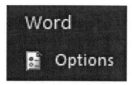

This is the **Options** command from the Backstage view.

3. Click on the box beside the text "Show Mini Toolbar on selection." This will remove or insert the checkmark, like a toggle switch.

Here's a picture of the Word Options dialog box. The very first command toggles the Mini Toolbar on and off. Click on the checkbox to deselect it if you don't want the Mini Toolbar appearing when you select text.

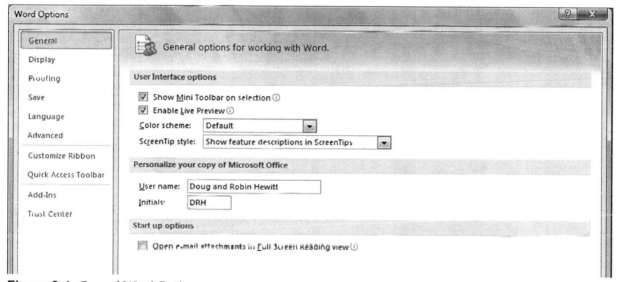

Figure 2-4. *General Word Options*

We'll return to the Word Options dialog box later. We wanted to introduce you to this important dialog box so that it will be familiar when we revisit it. You can jump ahead and search through Word Help for some of the options available here. Of course, we know some people might be distracted by the Mini Toolbar, so we wanted to show you how to turn it off.

For now, let's move on and look at how to do some basic text formatting.

Font Group

Let's take another look at the *Font* group. If you don't see it in your Ribbon, you might have to select the Home tab. That's the tab under which the Font group resides.

We'll list these *Font* group commands with a brief description of what the commands do. How do you change your text with these commands? After you select text in your document, go to the *Font* group and click on a command. View your document to see how it changes the look of the words. After a while, you might develop an artistic flair for making your words look aesthetically pleasing!

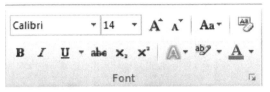

Here's a look at the *Font* group. Click on the *Home* tab is you don't see it.

We'll go briefly through some of the commands available with the font group. The best way to learn how to use these effects is to write some text, select the text, then click on a command.

Here are the commands in the top row of commands in the *Font* group.

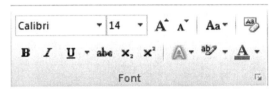

The first box has a drop down menu. Click on the arrowhead to open a menu and select a font.
The second box is the font size. We're using **14** here. Click on the arrowhead for a menu of choices.
The next two boxes are **Increase** font and **Decrease** font size (by 1 point).
Change your case options, upper and lower.
Clear formatting in the final command on the top row of the font group.

The second row of commands.
In order, you can make your text:
bold
italics
<u>underlined</u>
~~strikethrough~~
use subscript like H_2O
use superscript like $e = m c^2$
Use Text Effects (like shadows)
Highlight your text like you would with a highlighter pen
Change the font color

Have you ever wondered why the size of the font is given in units called points? It's a term that comes from the days when printers used typesets. The term stuck.

    The point size is the size of your text. One inch equals 72 points.

Let's take a moment to learn a new technique that's available with Word 2010, which has many new text effects available. When you select the command Text Effects, you'll be able to change your text to include the following effects.

- Outline
- Shadow
- Reflection
- Glow
- Bevel

Use your sample text (if you're following along with your computer) and find the *Font* group. Click on **Text Effects**.

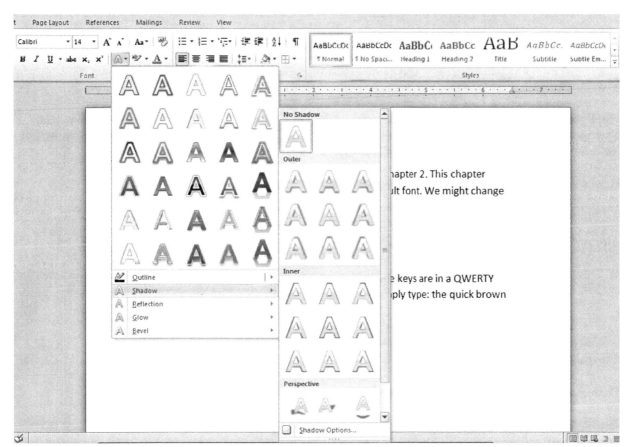

Figure 2-5. *Text Effects*

In our example, we have the **Shadow** command selected. As you can see, another menu opens up, giving you more commands to choose from. As you move your cursor over the choices, you can see in the background (your document) that your selected text will change to the command under the pointer. This is an effective way of seeing how a command choice will appear.

We're going to change some text to give you an idea of some of the command choices available to you and what they'll look like.

Outline, Shadow, Reflection, Glow, Bevel

Samples of text effects

The text effects command is one of the new features of Word 2010 that has lots of uses. In fact, we're going to spend the next chapter on Text Effects.

But for now, let's review the next group in the Ribbon under the *Home* tab, the *Paragraph* group.

Paragraph Group

The Paragraph group is the group to the right of the Font group. Later in this book, we'll show you how you can customize Ribbons, so you'll be able to change this arrangement if that's your desire, but for now let's go with the default Ribbon layout.

Here's what the default Paragraph group looks like.

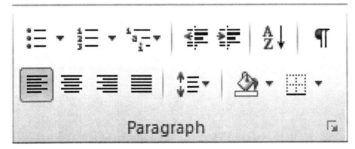

Figure 2-6. *The Paragraph Group*

There are three basic commands you need to know in the Paragraph group.

The first command is actually a set of command involving *justification*, which means your text is left or right justified (aligned with the left or right side of the page) or centered on the page. The other two commands you should be familiar with are:

Line spacing. Your English teacher might want your essay double or single spaced.
Indent. Your teacher might want the first line of your paragraph indented. The typical indent is 0.5 inch.

Paragraph Group Commands

We suggest you have a document open (maybe the practice text!) and try out each command. Look at how each command affects the text. If there's a command you want to investigate more, click on Word Help and type the command into the search box.

 Remember – the command you select will affect the text you have selected. Select your text before clicking on the command.

- Bullets
- Numbering
- Multilevel List
- Decrease Indent
- Increase Indent
- Sort
- Show/Hide ¶

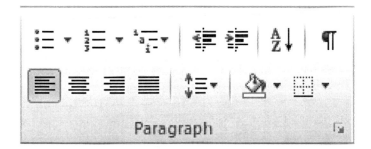

Paragraph

What do these commands do? Let's take a brief look

Bullets. Starts a bulleted list. Select text first to create a bulleted list.

Numbering. Starts a numbered list. Select text first to create a numbered list.

Multilevel List. Starts a multilevel list.

Decrease Indent. Decreases the indent of the paragraph.

Increase Indent. Increases the indent of the paragraph.

Sort. Sorts a list alphabetically or numerically.

Show/Hide ¶. Toggles between showing and hiding formatting marks such as the paragraph mark (shown).

Second Row, Paragraph Group Commands

- Align Text Left
- Center
- Align Text Right

- Line Spacing
- Shading
- Borders and Shading

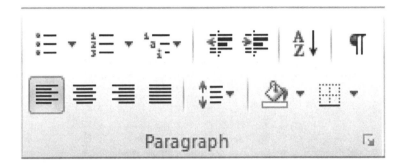

What about this second row of Paragraph group commands?

Let's take a brief look.

The first three buttons are the **Justification** buttons (left, right, centered, and left and right).
Line Spacing. This button selects line spacing. Select the down arrowhead to open a dialog box. Select the line spacing from the dialog box.

Shading. This puts a highlight color behind selected text.
Borders. This is a borders and gridlines button. With this button, you can add borders to tables, view table gridlines, and open the **Borders and Shading** Dialog Box.
Launcher. This is the little angled arrow box in the lower right corner of the Paragraph group. It launches a menu of commands.

The Paragraph group affects paragraphs, of course, and as such it is aptly named. But it's good to remember that paragraphs are composed of text. And when you select commands that affects paragraphs, they affect text. In that sense, of the commands on the Ribbon affect text in one way or another.

Styles

The next group on the Ribbon under the *Home* tab is the *Styles* group.

Figure 2-7. *The Styles Group*
The Styles buttons allow you to select preset ways to present your text. For example, if you're writing a term paper, you would want the title of the paper in a different style from the rest of the text.

There's a command for **Title**.
 You might divide your paper into sections such as Theory, Evidence, and Conclusion. These could be **Headings**.

Try typing "Conclusion" in a document. Highlight the word, then click on the different style commands to see how it changes the appearance of the word.
You can also change style with the **Change Styles** button.

Editing

The Editing group allows you to find words or phrases in your document, to replace text (or symbols or formatting) and to select text or objects or text with the same kind of formatting. With this command, you could select all bold text and make a change to that bold text.

Figure 2-8. *The Editing Group*

We'll go into these commands later. The **Find** command in Word 2010 has many new features. It opens a navigation pane that allows you to find what you're looking for. If you have a large document, this new feature will be a true time-saver and give you new techniques to work with.

Summary

In this chapter, we've shown you how to work with text in your document.

The Font groups is one of the primary groups in the Home Ribbon to work with text, but as we hope we've shown, all of the groups affect the text in one way or another.

One of the new techniques introduced in this chapter is **Text Effects**. We'll cover more of this important new group of commands in the next chapter. We've also hinted at new techniques that are possible with the Editing group via the Navigation pane. Don't worry; we will cover that as well. Stay tuned.

Chapter 3

■ ■ ■

Text Effects

Introduction

One of the new features of Word 2010 is the **Text Effects** command.

Because this feature has so many different commands and settings, we're going to spend some time with it and show you some techniques.

One of the ways in which you can use these text effects features is when you want to make a sign. It could be a **Yard Sale** sign or a sign indicating that people should **Keep Out!** There are, of course, other uses for these text effects. You can use them when making *fliers* or producing *brochures*. They are eye-appealing text effects that allow your words to jump off the page and catch the attention of readers. In this chapter, we'll show you the menus and commands that are associated with the **Text Effects** command located in the *Font* group on the Ribbon under the *Home* tab.

We hope, by the way, that you are starting to become familiar with the terms that we use to identify the locations of these commands. In the same way that a position on the surface of the planet can be identified by a longitude, latitude, and altitude (*thank you, Mr. GPS!*), the command button we want to identify can be located by the tab under which the Ribbon resides, the group in the Ribbon, and sometimes the Launcher menu of commands.

Text Effects

Open a new (blank) document and type in some text you might want to use in a sign that you could print and tape to a wall or door.

Here is our example. Note we have moved our cursor to the **Text Effects** button in preparation for selecting it and a small popup box has appeared. The box describes what the command does.

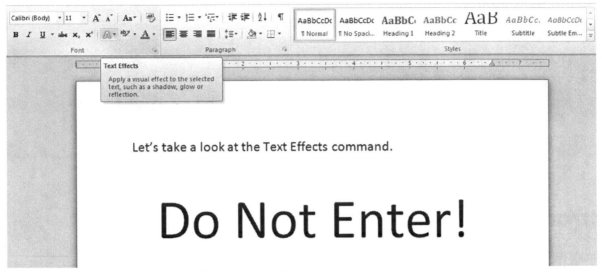

Figure 3-1. *Sample Text for Text Effects Command*

We are going to select "Do Not Enter!" and click on the **Text Effects** command. You will see a menu (or palette) of choices that will affect the way your text looks.

The palette choices represent different combinations of the text effects menu choices we'll cover in this chapter. These effects include, for example, the amount of shadowing you want to apply to your text. Let's go ahead and select **Text Effects** and move our cursor to one of the palette choices.

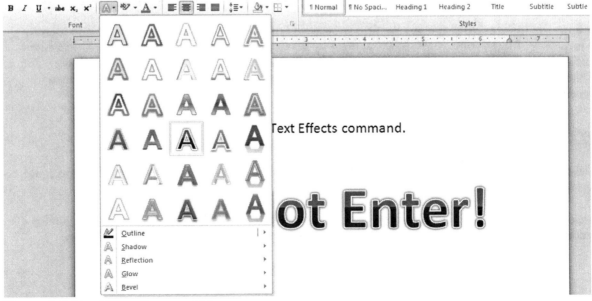

Figure 3-2. *Text Effects Command Menu*

You can see that there is a box around one of the capital letter A's in the menu of choices. This is where our cursor is pointing. Move your cursor over the various letters and you'll see the text in the background (in the document) change as you move your cursor. The current position of our pointer gives the text an outline effect.

See the bottom right corner in the matrix of A's? It looks like it has a shadow effect. That's because each of these letter A's is an illustration of what the command will do to your text.

Let's go ahead and select the bottom right A and see if we're right, that there will be a shadow effect to our text.

It helps to know what you want your text to look like when you're done, but it is also fun to explore some of the effects because they may produce an effect that you're not aware of.

Here's what we are looking at when we move our pointer over the bottom right A in the palette.

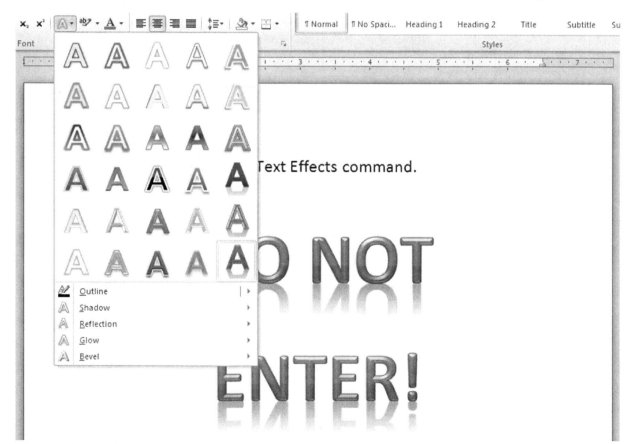

Figure 3-3. *Another Text Effect Selection*

Okay, we think you get the idea.

Let's move on and examine the effects that are available with the **Text Effects** command. If you look at the menu of commands below the palette of A's, you'll see that there are five effects to work with.

These effects open dialog boxes that present you with different command options.

- Outline
- Shadow
- Reflection
- Glow
- Bevel

Let's take a look at the options that are available with each of these commands.

Outline

Highlight your text and click on the **Outline** button. Note that your text does not change until you make selections, unlike moving your pointer of the palette of A's.

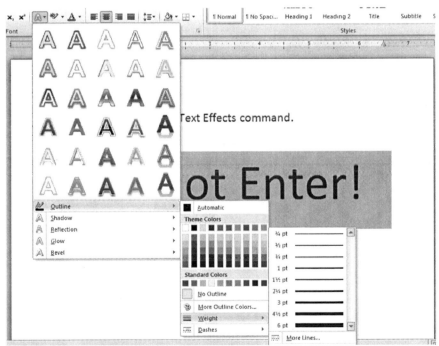

Figure 3-4. *Outline Options in Text Effects*

With this command, you can see that you can select the thickness (weight) of the line that will be the outline of your text. You can also select the color of the outline. You can also create dashed lines with your outlines.

Note that once you make selections with the colors, weight of the lines, and the dashed line effects, you have to go back to the palette of A's and select one of them.

We've selected a thick (3 point) outline effect.

Figure 3-5. *Do Not Enter with Outline Options*

Shadow

Click on **Text Effects.**, the click on **Shadow**.

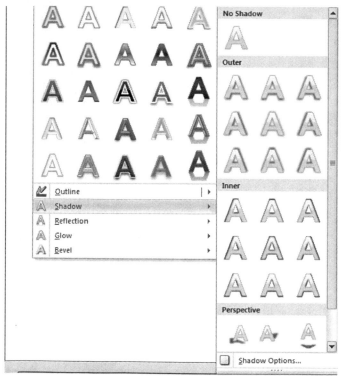

Figure 3-6. *Shadow Command*

You'll see that you have more A's to choose from!
(*Students will want to insert these into their report cards.*)

These A's are associated with different kinds of shadowing effects. First, notice that the first choice is **No Shadow**. Why does Word 2010 give you this option? Because in the palette of A's, there are combinations of text effects. You might like one of the choices but be thinking *if only it didn't have the shadow effect*. Well, here is where you would turn it off.

The other options for the shadowing effects allow you to have:

- **Inner** shadow effects
- **Outer** shadow effects
- **Perspective** shadow effects

You may have noticed that when you click on **Shadow** and the new command pane opens, there's another command available at the bottom called **Shadow Options** ....

Click on **Shadow Options** ....

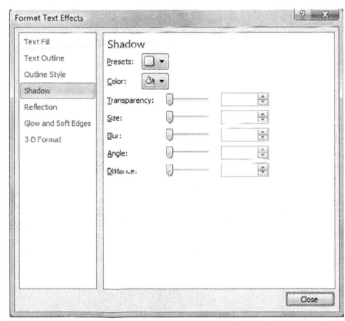

Figure 3-7. *More Shadow Options*

As you can see, this gives you options for changing the shadow effects. The qualities of the shadow that you can change can be selected from a list of presets, or you can choose them yourself. They include:

- Color
- Transparency
- Size
- Blur

- Angle
- Distance

Let's move on to the next **Text Effects** command, which is **Reflection**.
Reflection

To access the **Reflection** commands:

1) Click on **Text Effects**.
2) Click on **Reflection**.

You'll see another palette of choices that give you a visual representation of the **Reflection** qualities you can change. You can choose **No Reflection** or a number of different **Reflection** variations. Or, as with the **Shadow** command, you can click on **Reflection Options ...**.

If you click on **Reflection Options ...**, you are presented with a menu of commands. You can select from a menu of present values or you can choose to modify the reflection characteristics yourself.

You may want to stick with preset values until you begin to feel comfortable with how these different characteristics alter the way the text looks onscreen and on the printed page. Of course, we encourage experimentation!

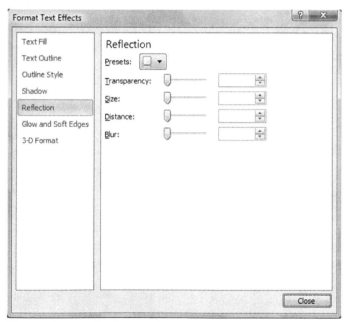

Figure 3-8. *Reflection Variations*

Along with the preset choices (a drop-down menu), you can alter the following characteristics:

- Transparency
- Size
- Distance
- Blur

Let's move to the next command in the **Text Effects** command choices. This command is called **Glow**. Glow

To access the **Glow** commands:

1) Click on **Text Effects**.
2) Select **Glow**.

A pop-up menu gives you a palette of choices with preset values. You can also select more colors from this menu. These are the color choices for the glow. You can also select **Glow Options** ….

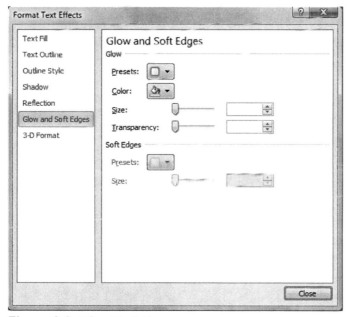

Figure 3-9. *Glow Variations*

Along with the preset choices (a drop-down menu), you can alter the following characteristics:

- Color
- Size
- Transparency
- Soft Edges

Let's move to the next command in the **Text Effects** command choices. This command is called **Bevel**.

A bevel is a slanting edge.
The Bevel variations can be subtle, depending on your font. But this command can add to the effect you're trying to achieve. It gives you one more tool with which to shape your text.

Bevel

To access the **Bevel** commands:

> 1) Click on **Text Effects**.
> 2) Select **Bevel**.

A pop-up menu gives you a palette of choices with preset values.

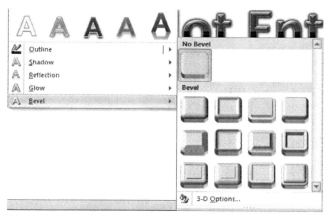

Figure 3-10. *Bevel Command*

From here, you can select **3-D Options** ....

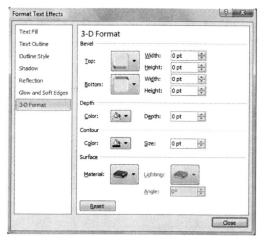

Figure 3-11. *3-D Options*

The **3-D Options** command allows you to change the point size of the top or bottom bevel. You can also change the depth color and point size. You can change the contour color and point size. You can also change the material appearance, lighting, and angle. A **Reset** button allows you change the values to the default values.

Summary

We spent an entire chapter working with the **Text Effects** command because it is a major new feature of Microsoft Word 2010.

With this command, you can change the way your text appears, both on your computer monitor and on the printed page. You can use **Text Effects** to enhance the shadowing, outline, glow, reflection, and bevel of your text. Various sub-menus offer you choices of changing the variables associated with each effect.

These **Text Effect** variations all have present values, and there is a preset palette of different combinations of these effects. The palette of A's gives you a visual presentation of how each selection will affect your selected text.

Chapter 4

■ ■ ■

Paragraph Techniques

Introduction

We've shown you how to go to the Backstage view and create documents and work with text. We've shown you the groups on the Ribbon under the *Home* tab.

You might remember the *Paragraph* group is in that Ribbon.

We've introduced you to the commands in the *Paragraph* group, but it such an important group in shaping your text and documents that we're going to delve more deeply into the available commands in this chapter.

There will also be an opportunity to explore other features in Word 2010 in this chapter, such as the new **Paste** features for text.

Understanding the commands in the *Paragraph* group, which are formatting commands (for the most part), will help give you a greater degree of confidence in working with documents. We'll cover those *Paragraph* commands in this chapter. We're going to also throw in a few other commands that we most often use. These commands that can save you a lot of time such as the **Undo** command. We will show you how to use the Quick Access Toolbar, which is available no matter which tab you select.

Word Help

We're going to show you where you can go for help for working with *Microsoft Word 2010*, other than this book, of course.

- Open *Microsoft Word 2010*.
- Open a blank document.

Now, look in the upper right corner of your screen. You'll see a small button with a question mark in it. This is the **Microsoft Office Word Help** button.

    The **Microsoft Office Word Help** button.

Click on the button and a dialog box appears.

Figure 4-1. *Microsoft Office Word Help Dialog Box*

Simply type the topic into the white box and hit **enter** or **Search**. You'll be shown instructions and explanations for the topic you entered. You can also click on the topics shown in the dialog box to access information on those topics.

 Type your topic in the form of a question, such as "how to add page numbers" to help Word identify your specific need.

Also note the book icon in the top menu bar.

This icon opens up another pane, the *Table of Contents*, which lists major search topics. You can search through the listed topics or type your question or subject here. There will also be a menu bar at the top of *Word Help*. These give you some basic commands to navigate *Word Help*.

- Back
- Forward
- Stop
- Refresh
- Home
- Print
- Change Font Size
- Show Table of Contents
- Keep on Top

Quick Access Toolbar

While we're on the subject of helping you to work with Microsoft Word 2010, let's take a moment to review the Quick Access Toolbar. Open Word 2010 if you're at your computer and look at the upper left portion of your screen. Beside the Office Button, you'll see a short row of command buttons. This is the *Quick Access Toolbar*. For now, we're going to show you the existing commands on this toolbar, but in a later chapter we'll show you how to add the commands that you use most frequently. Having your often used commands in one toolbar can definitely be a time-saver.

The *Quick Access Toolbar*.

Let's see what each of these command buttons do.

This is the **Save** button. If you've already saved your document once, it will save it with the same name and file format. If it's a new document and you haven't saved it yet, it opens the **Save As** dialog box so you give your document a name and select a file type.

This is the **Undo** command. It reverses your latest action. If you accidently perform a command, select **Undo** to correct your mistake.

This is the **Redo** (pronounced *re-dew*) command. If you made a mistake by selecting **Undo**, select **Redo** to repeat the action that you undid. It can also be referred to as the **Repeat** command.

If you're unfamiliar with the Undo and Redo (or Repeat) commands, now is a good time to try them out. Remember, performing these actions, clicking on commands, actually working with text in a document in Word 2010 is the best way to remember the techniques. It will help you to save time when working with Word, and you will eventually earn the envy of your coworkers and fellow students.

Try out the **Undo** and **Redo** buttons!

1. Open a new document and type a short sentence.
2. Select a word from your sentence by using the clicking and dragging with your mouse.
3. Delete the word by pressing the **delete** key. The word disappears.
4. Select **Undo** from the *Quick Access Toolbar*. Your word reappears in your sentence.
5. Select **Redo** to automatically perform the deletion again.
6. Select **Undo** one last time to get your deleted word back again.

The Paragraph Group

We've already gone over a few commands, those that are associated with the justification of text such as right justified or left justified, in the *Paragraph* group. Now we're ready to show you the rest.

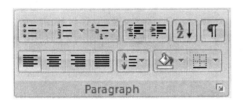

The *Paragraph* group. It's under the *Home* tab and is beside the *Font* Group.

Let's take a look at each command in this group. We'll summarize how the command affects your selected text. Then we'll perform a little exercise to help you to understand how these commands can help you to work with Word 2010. Knowing the commands and being familiar with them will help you with new Word techniques.

Paragraph **Group Commands**

Bullets. Starts a bulleted list. Select text first to create a bulleted list. Click on the icon to select from different types of bullets

Numbering. Starts a numbered list. Select text first to create a numbered list. Click on icon and you will see examples to choose from.

Multilevel List. Starts a multilevel list, which can include both numbers and letters. Think about those Roman Numeral outlines!

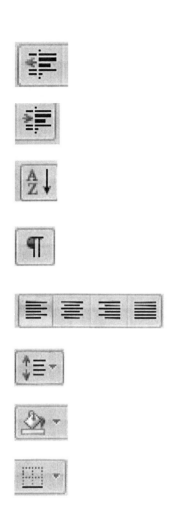

Decrease Indent. Decreases the paragraph indent.

Increase Indent. Increases the indent of the paragraph.

Sort. Sorts a list alphabetically or numerically.

Show/Hide ¶. Toggles between showing and hiding formatting marks such as the paragraph mark (shown). This will also show page breaks, section breaks, and spacing marks

These are the **Justification** buttons (left, right, and centered). This command aligns your selected text on the page, left, right, or centered.

Line Spacing. Select the down arrowhead to open a dialog box. You can double or single space, or select other spacing.

Shading. This adds a highlight color behind the selected text.

Borders. You can add borders to tables, view table gridlines, and open the **Borders and Shading** Dialog Box.

Paragraph. Opens the *Paragraph* dialog box.

Now, open a new blank document.

Let's type in some text to work with. Remember, we're going to be working with paragraph commands. In Word 2010 terms, the end of a paragraph occurs as you are typing text and press the **enter** key.

Type the following text.

> 1) This is the first line in my list.
> 2) This is the second line in my list.
> 3) This is the third line.
> 4) The fourth.
> 5) The fifth and final line in my list.

Here is what your Word 2010 document should look like.

This is the first line in my list.

This is the second line in my list.

This is the third line.

The fourth.

The fifth and final line in my list.

Figure 4-2. *Five Text Lines for a List*

Select the five text lines (or, you could call them paragraphs because you pressed **enter** after each line). Your text becomes highlighted.

This is the first line in my list.

This is the second line in my list.

This is the third line.

The fourth.

The fifth and final line in my list.

Figure 4-3. *Selecting Your Five Text Lines*

Now, select the **Bullets** command in the *Paragraph* group. Click your I-beam cursor somewhere in the document to de-select the text. Your page should now have a bulleted list.

- This is the first line in my list.
- This is the second line in my list.
- This is the third line.
- The fourth.
- The fifth and final line in my list.

Figure 4-4. *Bulleted List*

Now, select the five lines again. Select **Numbering** in the *Paragraph* group. Click your I-beam cursor somewhere in the text to de-select the text. Your page should have a numbered list.

1. This is the first line in my list.

2. This is the second line in my list.

3. This is the third line.

4. The fourth.

5. The fifth and final line in my list.

Figure 4-5. *Numbered List*

Now, let's say we want to center our list on the page and to bring the lines closer together in single line spacing.

1) Select the five lines.
2) Click on the **Center** button in the *Paragraph* group.
3) Click on the downward arrowhead in the **Line Spacing** command button.
4) Select **1.0** for single spacing.

If you're following along, you'll notice that your lines might not be as close together as you'd expect for single spacing. That's because Word can add space automatically after a paragraph mark, or when your press **enter**.

Select the **Paragraph** command arrow in the bottom right corner of the *Paragraph* group. You'll see the following.

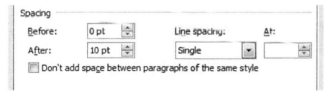

Figure 4-6. *Spacing Commands in Paragraph dialog box*

Note that the *Line Spacing* is set at *Single* because that's the result of our selection at the **Line Spacing** command button. But there is "*10 pt*" added after each of our paragraphs, or whenever we press **enter**.

1) Select the downward facing arrowhead beside the "*10 pt*".
2) Press twice to select "*0 pt*".
3) Click on **OK**.
4) Click your cursor somewhere on the page to de-select the text.

Your list should now look like ours.

1. This is the first line in my list.
2. This is the second line in my list.
3. This is the third line.
4. The fourth.
5. The fifth and final line in my list.

Figure 4-7. *Numbered List, Centered*

If you decide that you don't want your list to be a numbered list, select the lines of text and click on the **Numbering** command again.

We suggest clicking on the **Bullets** command and then the **Left Justify** command so that you can follow along with the changes we're making to our document as we write.

Paragraphs

What is a paragraph?

Many of us can remember some vague high school English definition of a set of sentences that are related to each other. For *Learning New Techniques with Microsoft Word 2010*, it is useful to think of a paragraph as the lines of text the go before the paragraph mark symbol (and after the previous paragraph mark). The paragraph mark symbol looks like this: ¶.

Click on the **Show/Hide ¶** command. This is the button that has the symbol ¶. Your document will be dotted with paragraph mark symbols, one for every time you pressed **enter**.

Hide your paragraph mark symbols by clicking on the **Show/Hide ¶** again, noting that this commands acts like a toggle switch, turning the symbols on and off.

Changing Paragraph Properties

We're going to show you how to change the properties of paragraphs in your text, which will change how your text appears on the page.

In order to show you how to change paragraph properties, we need some text to work with. We'll write some sample text that we'll call *My First Class Essay*. You can write your own text or use a file you've already written and have saved on your computer.

My First Class Essay
by Jill or John Q. Public

This is the first paragraph of our essay. We started out with our title, hit return, then added a byline. Then

we added an extra return in order to give us some space between paragraphs.

As you can see, we haven't really said much of anything yet. That's because we're trying to pad the word

count. We'll write about how to find the word count later. (Hint: look at the lower left portion of the

screen.)

Now we're on our third and final paragraph. Because this is an English essay, we would like to point out

that all of the letters of the alphabet appear in the sentence: The quick brown fox jumped over the lazy

dog.

Figure 4-8. *My First Class Essay Sample Text*

We're going to make changes to all of the paragraphs in *My First Class Essay*. What we want to do is change all of the line spacing to single spacing with no extra space after the end of any of the paragraphs. We also want to indent the first line of each paragraph.

How do we make these changes? They're easy to do now that you understand how paragraphs appear in your document.

To make the paragraph changes:

Click your I-beam cursor in your document.
Press **ctrl** and **a** at the same time to "select all" of the text in your document (this is a keyboard shortcut).

Click on the **Paragraph** command in the lower right corner of the *Paragraph* group. A dialog box appears.

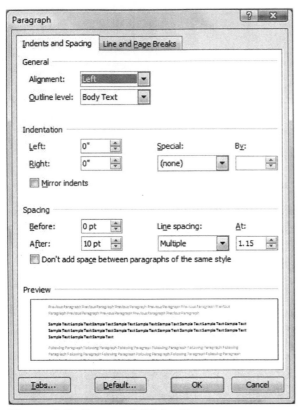

Figure 4-9. *Paragraph Dialog Box*

In the *Indentation* section, click on the down arrow under "*Special:*"

Select **First Line**. Notice the "*By:*" amount goes to 0.5 inches. That's a good indentation amount, but this is the place to change it if you later decide that a smaller or larger indentation is your preference. Click on the down arrow under *Line Spacing:*

Select **Single**. Note that this is where to change line spacing in your document.

 Remember, the changes you make in the *Paragraph* dialog box will affect the selected text. If you open a new document, you can make these selections initially, then all of your text will follow the selected format.

Click on the selection arrows beside "*After:*" under *Line Spacing:* and select 0 pt. Click on **OK**.

You might have noticed one particular feature of *Paragraph* dialog box, namely, the *Preview* pane. When you make a change in the *Paragraph* dialog box, going from double spacing to single spacing for example, the sample text in the *Preview* pane gives you a preview of the effect of your selection.

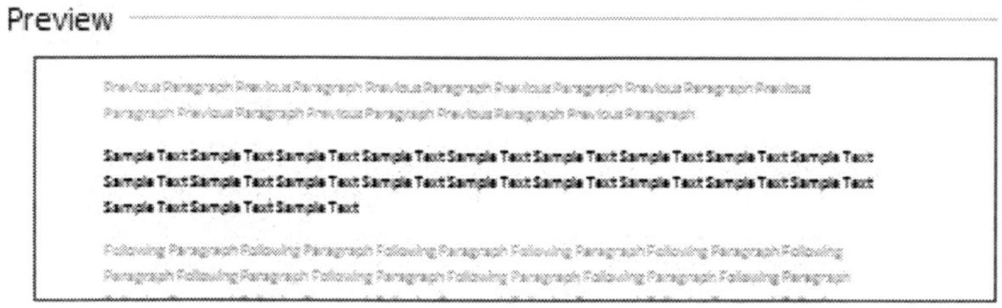

Preview

Figure 4-10. *Preview Pane*

Our document looks like the one below. Don't forget to go to *Backstage view* to save your document. Remember, you can go back to your document, select different portions of text, and try different line spacing formats and different commands in the *Paragraph* dialog box. Practicing with *Word 2010* commands will help you to locate them later, when you need them.

If you haven't centered your title and byline, select them in your *My First Class Essay* document, then click on **Center Justification**.

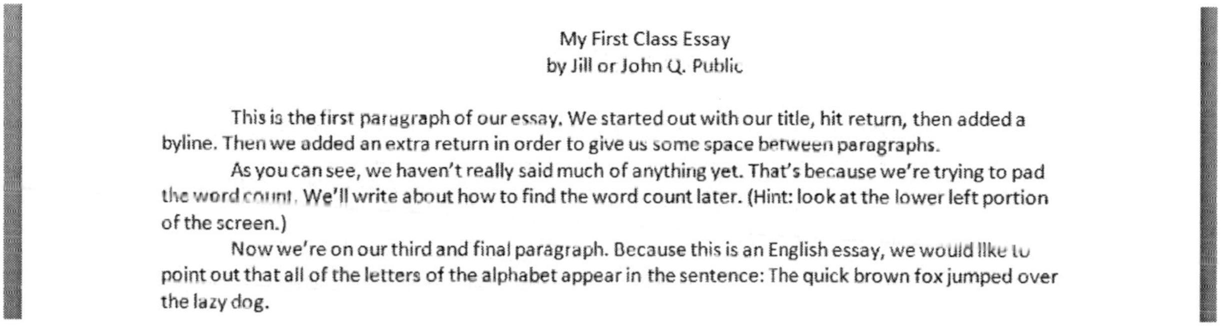

My First Class Essay
by Jill or John Q. Public

This is the first paragraph of our essay. We started out with our title, hit return, then added a byline. Then we added an extra return in order to give us some space between paragraphs.

As you can see, we haven't really said much of anything yet. That's because we're trying to pad the word count. We'll write about how to find the word count later. (Hint: look at the lower left portion of the screen.)

Now we're on our third and final paragraph. Because this is an English essay, we would like to point out that all of the letters of the alphabet appear in the sentence: The quick brown fox jumped over the lazy dog.

Figure 4-11. *Single Spacing and Indented First Lines*

Paragraph Tidbits

We're going to save some of the commands in the Paragraph dialog box, which appears when you select the **Paragraph Launcher** command in the lower right corner of the *Paragraph* group, for later. The **Tabs** command is one of those.

When you select the Paragraph Launcher command, you'll notice that there is a dialog box with two tabs: *Indents and Spacing* and *Line and Page Breaks*.

Line and Page Breaks is a tab selection that allows you to select options for how your paragraphs behave when they occur near the bottom of the page. For example, you might want to keep your entire paragraph on the same page so that half of it isn't on the bottom of one page and the other half is on the top of the next page. In that case, you would check the box **Window/Orphan control**.

Back on the *Indents and Spacing* tab, note that you can increase (or decrease) the indention of the lines of text. Simple click on the increase and decrease arrows in the *Indentation* section.

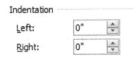

Indentation section. Increase and decrease the left and right margins here.

These perform the same functions as the **Decrease Indent** and **Increase Indent** command buttons in the Paragraph group.

Decrease Indent. Decreases the indent of the paragraph.

Increase Indent. Increases the indent of the paragraph.

Summary

This chapter focused on the paragraph. We covered commands in the *Paragraph* group, and also the commands that are available when the *Paragraph* dialog box is opened via the **Paragraph Launcher** command. These commands included those that change the way your text appears in a document, including line spacing, indentation, and margins. We showed you how to indent the first line of every paragraph.

We also covered bulleted lists and numbered lists in this chapter. These lists are great ways for your documents to have a better visual impact.

We also showed you how to access *Microsoft Office Word Help*. With *Word 2010*, the Help command is more integrated with the other Microsoft Office applications.

The *Quick Access Toolbar* was covered in this chapter, including the **Undo** and **Redo** commands. Remember, **Undo** is an essential command for correcting mistakes. The word has crept into our vocabulary. In our daily lives, we are always looking to *undo* our errors.

It might be useful at this point to review the commands that have been discussed so far in this book. Once you know these commands well, you'll be able to create, open, and save documents. You'll be able to change the font and the appearance of your paragraphs. You can make bulleted lists and undo any mistakes you make while working with your document.

In other words, you'll be on your way to becoming proficient at using *Word 2010*.

Chapter 5

■ ■ ■

Techniques with Pages

Introduction

We've worked with basic page layouts so far.

These basic layouts are great for most purposes. You can use them for letters, resumes, or class essays. But sometimes you'll want to work more with the layout of the text on the page. In this chapter, we're going to show you different ways to position the page and to put text on the page.

We're also going to use this chapter to show you how to use the ruler. It's an easy and visual way to set the margins for your text. You can also set different margins for different sections of text. For essay papers that are quoting long passages, the ability to set larger margins for quoted material will help make writing term papers a breeze.

We'll also work with tabs. They are preset positions on the ruler that align the text. Text can be centered on tabs, aligned to the left of a tab, or aligned to the right of a tab.

Tab leaders are also covered in this chapter. They're a great way to guide readers to visually follow along with your text.

The Ruler

Think of the ruler as one of those old fashioned wooden rulers laid down across the top of your page. The typical piece of paper that *Word 2010* uses (and most printers have as a default setting) is 8-½ inches wide and 11 inches long.

When you open a new document, your ruler might not be displayed. It's a checkbox that needs to be checked. To view the ruler, click on the *View* tab.

Look at the *Show* group. Click on the box beside **Ruler** to add a checkmark.

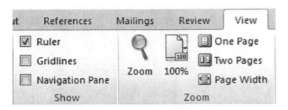

Put a checkmark in the **Ruler** checkbox in order to show the ruler when working on your document.

Now, when you look at your blank document, you should see a bar with numbers on it above the top of your document. These numbers represent inches, and they will help you to set margins in your text.

Figure 5-1. *The Ruler*

As you can see in the ruler in Figure 4-1, the "0" mark in the ruler does not start at the edge of the page. The "0" mark starts 1 inch from the edge of the page. That's because the left margin is set at 1 inch. The right edge of the page is at the 7-½ inches mark. When you add the left margin of 1 inch, you get the 8-½ inch standard width of the page.

There's also a ruler on the left side of the document window, a vertical ruler, but we're not going to concern ourselves with that one for now. Instead, let's focus on the horizontal ruler at the top of your document.

Why all the fuss about inches and margins and rulers?

Because they will help you to understand other commands and tools in *Word 2010*. We're going to cover **Tabs** next, and the ruler will provide you an excellent visual tool to lay out text in the way you want.

For now, let's look at how we can set margins and indents using the ruler.

Setting Margins and Indents with the Ruler

If you want to follow along, type three paragraphs into a new document in which you have the ruler turned on. We're going to write three paragraphs of a class term paper in which our second paragraph is going to be a long quotation. We'll quote a couple of authors, namely, us.

Because this term paper might be turned in to be graded, we'll need to follow MLA style for direct quotes of long passages. Long quotations will need to be indented one inch from the normal left margin.

It's easy with the ruler.

Here are our three paragraphs in our class assignment.

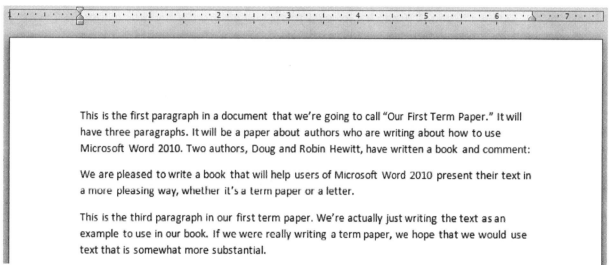

This is the first paragraph in a document that we're going to call "Our First Term Paper." It will have three paragraphs. It will be a paper about authors who are writing about how to use Microsoft Word 2010. Two authors, Doug and Robin Hewitt, have written a book and comment:

We are pleased to write a book that will help users of Microsoft Word 2010 present their text in a more pleasing way, whether it's a term paper or a letter.

This is the third paragraph in our first term paper. We're actually just writing the text as an example to use in our book. If we were really writing a term paper, we hope that we would use text that is somewhat more substantial.

Figure 5-2. *Our First Term Paper*

Now, if you look at the left end of the ruler, you'll see a downward pointing arrowhead and an upward pointing arrowhead, and the arrowheads are aligned. The top arrow indicates where the first line in a paragraph starts, and the arrowhead (pointer) below that indicates where the rest of the lines will be aligned.

These are called indent controls.

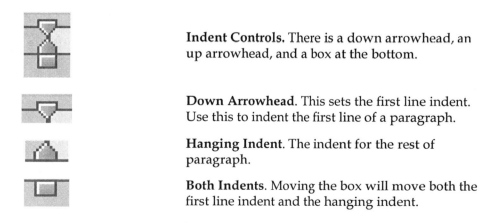

Indent Controls. There is a down arrowhead, an up arrowhead, and a box at the bottom.

Down Arrowhead. This sets the first line indent. Use this to indent the first line of a paragraph.

Hanging Indent. The indent for the rest of paragraph.

Both Indents. Moving the box will move both the first line indent and the hanging indent.

Let's set tasks using the three indent controls with the three paragraphs in our term paper. Here's what we want to do.

- Change the first line indent for the first paragraphs to 0.5".
- Move the entire second paragraph indent in 1.0".
- This will make the second paragraph an accepted MLS style for a quoted paragraph. Note that if we had multiple paragraphs in a long quotation, all of which would be indented 1.0", the paragraphs within the long indented quotation would additionally have first lines indented an additional 0.5".
- Leave the first line of the third paragraph with no indent, but indent the rest of the paragraph 0.5".

In order to change these indents, select the paragraph, then move the ruler's indent controls as needed for that paragraph. Select the next paragraph, and move the ruler's indents for that paragraph. You'll see that the indents will affect only the selected paragraph.

Let's see what your paragraphs and rulers should look like for each paragraph.

First Paragraph

After you've changed the indent controls for the first paragraph, your document should look like the figure that follows. Note the position of the indent controls. The text in the figure is still highlighted, which means the indent controls for that paragraph will show in the ruler.

This is the first paragraph in a document that we're going to call "Our First Term Paper." It will have three paragraphs. It will be a paper about authors who are writing about how to use Microsoft Word 2010. Two authors, Doug and Robin Hewitt, have written a book and comment:

Figure 5-3. *First Line Indent at 0.5"*

Second Paragraph

After you've selected the second paragraph and changed the hanging indent, you should see a ruler and document like the one in the figure that follows. Note the position of the arrowhead indent pointers!

This is the first paragraph in a document that we're going to call "Our First Term Paper."
It will have three paragraphs. It will be a paper about authors who are writing about how to use
Microsoft Word 2010. Two authors, Doug and Robin Hewitt, have written a book and comment:

We are pleased to write a book that will help users of Microsoft Word 2010
present their text in a more pleasing way, whether it's a term paper or a letter.

This is the third paragraph in our first term paper. We're actually just writing the text as an
example to use in our book. If we were really writing a term paper, we hope that we would use
text that is somewhat more substantial.

Figure 5-4. *Second Paragraph Hanging and First Line Indent at 1.0"*

Third Paragraph

After you've selected the third paragraph and changed both indents (by dragging the box), you should
have a document that looks like the following figure. Note the indent control positions in the ruler!

This is the first paragraph in a document that we're going to call "Our First Term Paper."
It will have three paragraphs. It will be a paper about authors who are writing about how to use
Microsoft Word 2010. Two authors, Doug and Robin Hewitt, have written a book and comment:

We are pleased to write a book that will help users of Microsoft Word 2010
present their text in a more pleasing way, whether it's a term paper or a letter.

This is the third paragraph in our first term paper. We're actually just writing the text as an
example to use in our book. If we were really writing a term paper, we hope that we
would use text that is somewhat more substantial.

Figure 5-5. *Third Paragraph Hanging Indent at 1.0"*

These exercises should give you a good feel for using the ruler and the indent controls. Note that you can select a paragraph and move the arrowhead at the right side of the ruler to change the left margin of your text.

Tabs

Look over to the left of the ruler, at the edge of the display. You'll see a small right angle in a box. This is the Tab control.

Click on the button to select different type of tabs. When you click your pointer on the ruler, a tab will appear. The type of tab that appears is the one that is show in this selection box.

A tab is a marker, a line in the sand, *per se*, and the words that you type as text will be aligned to the tab. Your text could be aligned to the left of the tab or to the right of the tab. There are other tab choices, too. Let's take a look.

Tab Selections

Left tab. This tab will be aligned to the left of the text, meaning that text will be to the right of it. Look at our previous *Term Paper* examples.

Center tab. The text you type after selecting this tab will be centered on the tab.

Right tab. This tab will be aligned to the right of the text, meaning that text will be to the left of it.

Decimal tab. Decreases the indent of the paragraph.

Bar Tab. This does not align text. It inserts a vertical bar at the position of the tab.

First Line Indent. This is not actually a tab, per se, but you can set the first line indent with this command. Another shortcut!

Hanging Indent. Again, not actually a tab. It's an alignment mark, though. Lines after the first line in a paragraph align to this mark.

Working With Tabs

So, how can the use of tabs help you work with *Word 2010*? The sky's the limit, but let's start with the realization that tabs are alignment tools. When you want aligned text, tabs are the tools you use to accomplish your goals.

Let's say that you want to start a birthday list. You might add to this list throughout the year as ideas occur to you. Making your list is easy with tabs.

John and Jill Q. Public have three children, whose names are Jeremy, Jill (named after her mother), and Jason.

They could make their list like this:

> *Jeremy: golf clubs, gift card …*
> *Jill: purse, free spa visit …*
> *Jason: bouncy ball, alphabet blocks …*

But here's how to set up an easy tab list.

1. Open a new document.
2. Type "Family Birthday List"
3. Type "Jeremy", "Jill", and "Jason". Separate each name with a space.

Here's what your document should look like.

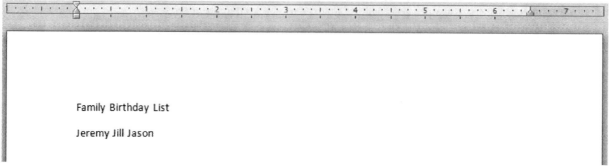

Figure 5-6. *Family Birthday List (before tabs)*

1. Next, select the first line (Family Birthday List) and click on the **Center** command in the *Paragraph* group.
2. Select the second line (Jeremy Jill Jason). With the text in the second line highlighted, click on the **Tab Control** until the *Center Tab* icon is shown.
3. Click on the ruler three times, at the 2" mark, the 3.5" mark, and the 5" mark.

Here's what your document should look like.

Figure 5-7. *Setting Three Center Tabs (second line only)*

Let's take a close-up look at the center tabs so you can see the alignment with the ruler markings.

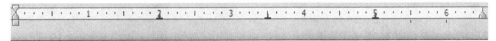

Figure 5-8. *Ruler With Three Center Tabs*

Now, we need to align our three names (Jeremy, Jill, and Jason) with the tab settings. But first we want to center "Family Birthday List" on the page. Let's do both!

1. Select the first line, Family Birthday List, and select **Center** in the *Paragraph* group.
2. Click your I-beam cursor in front of the J in Jeremy. Press **tab**.
3. Click your I-beam cursor in front of the J in Jill. Press **tab**.
4. Click your I-beam cursor in front of the J in Jason. Press **tab**.
5. It looks great, but we like for our "column" headers, the names of the birthday gift recipients, to stand apart, so let's underline them.
6. Select the line with Jeremy, Jill, and Jason in it.
7. Click on the **Underline** command in the Paragraph group.

Here's what your document should look like.

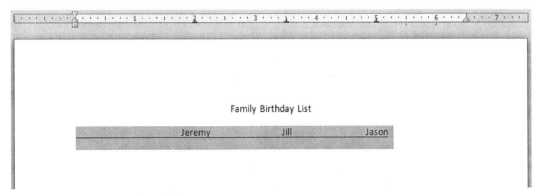

Figure 5-9. *Underlined Birthday List*

As you can see, the entire highlighted paragraph, or line of text, is underlined. This isn't what we wanted. We want only the words, which in this case are the names of our birthday gift recipients, underlined. So how do we change our Underline command to underline words only? Easy!

1. Click on the **Font Launcher** command in the lower right corner of the *Font* group to show the *Font* dialog box.
2. Click on the down arrow in the **Underline Style:** command to open a menu of choices.

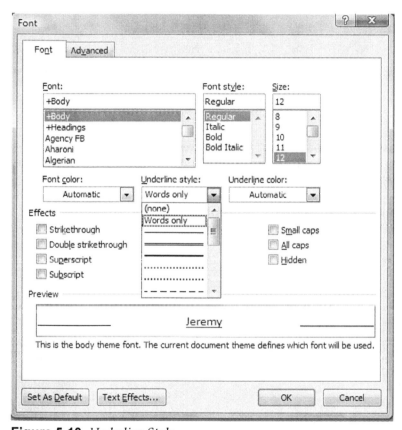

Figure 5-10. *Underline Style*

1. Select **Words only**.
2. Click elsewhere to deselect the text.

Here's what your document should look like.

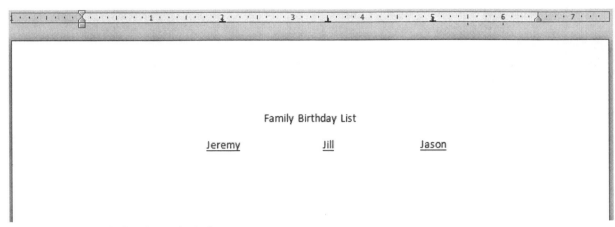

Figure 5-11. *Underlined Words Only*

Okay, now that you have your tabs set up, we're going to go to the next line below the line with the names of Jeremy, Jill, and Jason. If your insertion point (cursor) is at the end of the word Jason and you press **enter**, you'll go to the next line, but you'll still have underlining turned on.

 When the insertion point (typically, your I-beam cursor) is at the end of a paragraph and you press **enter**, the formatting of that paragraph will be carried over to the next paragraph.

If your underlining is turned on, turn it off by toggling the command. Do this by selecting the current line of text (the birthday gifts line) and selecting the **Underline** command in the *Paragraph* group. Now, we're ready to enter the presents for the birthday list.

17. Press **tab** and type "golf clubs."
18. Press **tab** and type "purse."
19. Press **tab** and type "bouncy ball."
20. Press **enter**.
21. Press **tab** and type "gift card."
22. Press **tab** and type "free spa visit."
23. Press **tab** and type "alphabet blocks."
24. Press **enter**.

Make your title of "Family Birthday List" bold by selecting the line and selecting **Bold** from the *Font* group.

Here's what your document should look like.

Figure 5-12. *Family Birthday List*

As you can see, you now have a birthday list that is visually appealing. You can use the tab technique for other lists, including lists in class essays and term papers.

Remember, tabs are a great way to align text. You can use tabs, too, for other purposes. For example, if your cursor is in a table, pressing tab moves your cursor to the next cell in the table.

The type of tab selected can provide great visual tools to help you make your documents appealing. You can also use tab leaders.

Tab Leaders

Tab leaders are a way to automatically insert characters in front of a tab.

Let's add periods (or decimal points) between the gift items in our list of birthday presents.

With your *Family Birthday List* document open, select the **Paragraph Launcher** in the *Paragraph* group. In the lower left corner of the dialog box, select the **Tab** command. Another dialog box opens.

You should see the Tab dialog box with the three tab settings. If not, go back and make sure your insertion point is in the area of your document that has those tab settings. Your title will not show the tab settings.

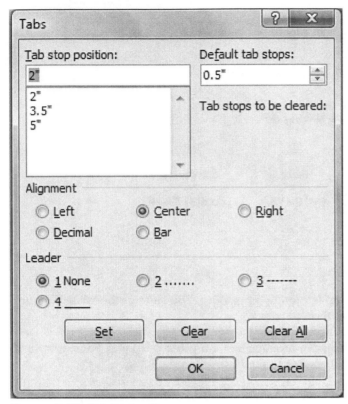

Figure 5-13. *Tab Dialog Box*

To set decimal point leaders for our second and third tab, use your cursor and click and drag to select the two lines of gifts. Then:

1. Select "**3.5"**" in the tab box.
2. Select the circle beside the row of dots to select it in the *Leader* section.
3. Click on **Set**.
4. Repeat Steps 1 – 3 for the "**5.0"**" tab.
5. Click on **OK**.

Here is how our list looks now.

Family Birthday List

Jeremy	Jill	Jason
Golf Clubs ....Purse ....Bouncey Ball
Gift Card ....Free Spa Visit.......... Alphabet Blocks

Figure 5-14. *Decimal Point Tab Leaders*

You can explore some of the other tab features, such as selecting a different leader, at your convenience. For now, let's move on to changing the layout of the page.

Page Layout

While much of our work uses the standard 8.5" by 11" page layout, there are times when we want the paper to be wider. By selecting a horizontal landscape for a page layout, we can have the effect of rotating the paper 90 degrees. One reason we might want to do this is to make a yard sale sign.

Follow these steps to create your yard sale sign.

1. Open *Word 2010.*
2. Select **New** from the *Backstage view.*
3. Select **Blank Document**.
4. Select the **Page Layout** tab.
5. Select **Orientation** in the *Page Setup* group.
6. Select **Landscape**.

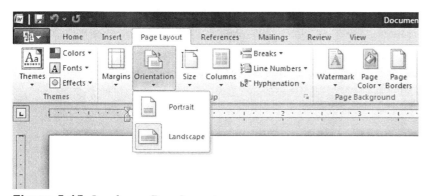

Figure 5-15. *Landscape Page Layout*

Note the width of the ruler above the document. The page is now 11" wide.

Now that we have the page laid out in a landscape format, let's type our yard sale text. Make your own text or type along with us.

1. Type "YARD SALE".
2. Press enter.
3. Type "Saturday at 9:00 AM".
4. Select the first line of text and select a font size of **72** in the *Font* group in the drop-down menu. (You might have to select the *Home* tab to access the *Font* group.)
5. Select the second line of text and select a font size of **48** from the drop-down menu.
6. Select both lines of text and select **Center** in the *Paragraph* group under the *Home* tab.

This works for all kinds of signs. You might, for example, want a DO NOT ENTER sign or DO NOT DISTURB. Here is what our sign looks like.

Figure 5-16. *Yard Sale Sign*

Use your creativity to come up with useful signs. We'll have ways to make your signs even more appealing later. For now, you can consider changing the color of your text in order to make it stand out more. This is a good time to explore **Text Effects**.

When selecting font size, you can use the drop-down menu or you can click in the box and type your own desire size into the box (then hit **enter**).

Summary

In this chapter, we showed you how to change the layout of your page. This is a great way to design your own signs. We also invited you to explore different ways signs can appear by using **Text Effects** on the text in your sign.

We also covered tabs, which can be accessed via the Paragraph Launcher under the Home tab in the Paragraph group. We showed you how to set tabs and the different kinds of tabs. Tabs are often useful in making lists. Tab leaders, such as periods (or decimal points), can help readers visually read along a horizontal line.

While we were talking about tabs, we discussed the ruler and how to set tabs there. The ruler is also a useful tool to set margins and indents.

While we were doing this, we wrote *Our Term Paper* and our *Family Birthday List*. And, of course, we ended up with a *YARD SALE* sign.

Chapter 6

■ ■ ■

Spelling, Grammar, and Review

Introduction

Now that you have some words on the page, we'll take a look at the spell checking and grammar checking capabilities of *Word 2010*. You can use these features to make sure you're using the right words and using them in the right way. In this chapter, we'll show you how to check the spelling in your document and the grammar of your text. We'll also look at some of the automatic formatting features.

We're also going to cover some of the review features of Word 2010. When you write a document and send it to someone else for review, you can track the changes that were made to your document. This can be valuable, especially if more than one person is going to make changes to your document because Word will let you know who made a particular change.

Back to spelling …, we'll delve into the automatic correction feature, which corrects text as you type. You might not even be aware of some of the changes that the automatic correction feature performs! This is a book designed to help you make better documents with *Microsoft Word 2010*, and there are some how-to books that will explain spell checking far into the advanced chapters. That's a shame, because it is a feature that is very basic, although it requires some degree of explanation in order to use it properly. And the same goes for grammar checking. Still, if you're looking to produce a document that has no spelling errors and is grammatically correct, the features in this chapter are essential.

So, let's get to work!

Automated

Spell checking can be performed in two ways. You can wait until your document is finished and then select the **Spelling & Grammar** command to check the document, or you can have *Word 2010* automatically check for spelling and grammar as you type. When a spelling error occurs, a red squiggly line will appear under the misspelled word. For grammar checking, a green squiggly line will appear beneath the word or words in question.

For some people, having their typing interrupted by squiggly lines can be distracting. They prefer to write full steam ahead and check for spelling and grammar later. Others like to correct errors as they go. Maybe they worry that they'll forget to check the spelling, which has certainly happened in many office settings.

Let's look at where you can find the commands to turn automated spelling and grammar checking on or off:

1. Open a new document.
2. Click on the **Microsoft Office** button.
3. Select the **Word Options** button near the bottom of the pane.
4. A dialog pane opens. Select **Proofing** in the left menu column.
5. The *Proofing* dialog box opens.

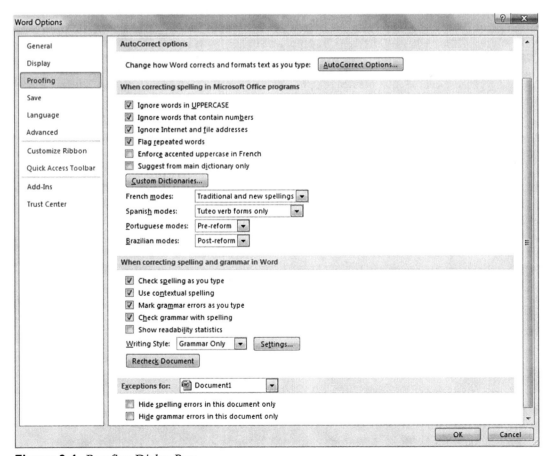

Figure 6-1. *Proofing Dialog Box*

There are a number of options we can select from the menu. For now, let's look at the automatic spelling and grammar checkboxes. These are the options that appear under the header bar titled *When correcting spelling and grammar in Word*.

These checkbox options can be seen in the following figure.

When correcting spelling and grammar in Word

☑ Check spelling as you type
☑ Use contextual spelling
☑ Mark grammar errors as you type
☑ Check grammar with spelling
☐ Show readability statistics

Writing Style: | Grammar Only | ▼ | | Settings... |

Recheck Document

Figure 6-2. *When correcting spelling and grammar in Word Dialog Box*

If you don't want the spelling and grammar checking to happen while you're typing, simply uncheck the boxes for *Check spelling as you type* and *Mark grammar errors as you type*.

Contextual spelling can help you to catch words that are spelled correctly for one meaning of the word, but it might not be the meaning you want to use. This can be helpful for people who aren't sure about the spellings of certain words.

Here's an example of when contextual spelling can catch a mistake. Contextual spelling errors appear as a squiggly blue line below the word in question.

Jack and Jill went for a walk over their.

The word *their* is spelled correctly, but not in this context. The spelling should be *there*.

It should be noted that *Word* doesn't always get it right. That's why their suggested corrections are always *suggestions*. Use common sense when looking at suggested corrections. If you're not sure, ask for help or try finding your answer on the Internet.

 If you want to look for more help than is found in *Word Help*, there are many Internet sites with help for working with *Word*. Use a search engine and type in your question. Also, the Microsoft website has excellent help features. Search for "Microsoft Word Help" and you'll find it.

If you turn off automatic spelling and grammar checking (by removing the checks from the checkboxes in *Word Options – Proofing*), you can still check them after you're finishing writing. Simply click on the *Review* tab.

The *Review* Ribbon appears.

Figure 6-3. *The Review Ribbon*

We'll go over the review capabilities later in this chapter. Note, though, there is a Tracking group, which allows you to track changes made to your document. You can also insert comments with the New Comment command in the Comments group.

In the Proofing group, the left-most group, you'll see the Spelling & Grammar command.

 Click on the **Spelling & Grammar** button in the *Proofing* group under the *Review* tab to spell check and grammar check your document.

If you click on the **Spelling & Grammar** button, *Word* will progress through your document and ask you about each potential spelling or grammar error. In our example, *Word 2010* notes that there could be a possible word choice error and highlights the word *their* in blue.

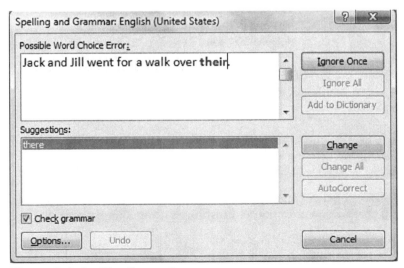

Figure 6-4. *Spelling Suggestions*

The *Spelling and Grammar* dialog box suggests a spelling of *there* in the *Suggestions* box. If you want to take the suggestion, select the **Change** button. You can also select the **Ignore Once** button to ignore this single occurrence of the error. If the word or phrase in error occurs in multiple locations in the document, you'll also have the choice to select the **Ignore All** (occurrences) button.

You can also reach the *Word Options* dialog box by selecting the **Options** button in the lower left corner of the *Spelling and Grammar* dialog box. That's where you can select the *Proofing* pane and choose the checkboxes for automatic spelling and grammar checking (see Figure 5-1).

Automated Options

If you're typing text with the automatic spell and grammar checker turned on, the squiggly lines will appear in your document as you type them. But how do you access the dialog box with the suggested change?

Easy, just right click on the word in question.
Let's run through an example. We're going to purposefully misspell words and make a grammar error in the following sentence:

> *The rain in Spain stays mainly on the plain.*

Only we're going to type it like this:

> *The rain in Spain stay mainly on the plane.*

The words *rain in Spain stay* earns a squiggly line. When we right click anywhere in the words above the squiggly line, we get the following pop-up dialog boxes. Note that our mini-toolbar appears also.

Figure 6-5. *Grammar Suggestions*

You can see at the top of the grammar box that *Word* is suggesting two changes because the noun (*rain*) does not agree with the verb (*stay*). Either the *rains* have to stay or the *rain stays*. For our purpose, we would choose the first suggestion. Choose the first line by clicking on it, and *Word* makes the correction in our document.

 You may also have some Paste options when you right click on the squiggly line. This allows you to paste any text you have copied or cut and **Keep Source Formatting**, **Merger Formatting**, or paste **Text only**.

There are some other options with the pop-up grammar box.

Ignore Once. This will cause *Word* to ignore this one occurrence of the grammar error.

Grammar ... This opens the *Grammar* dialog box.

About this sentence. This opens a *Help* box that describes the applicable grammar rule.

Look up ... This opens a *Research* box that offers to find articles on the Internet about the word or words selected (more info follows).

Paste. This inserts text (or pictures) from the clipboard. Whatever you copied (or cut) last will be inserted.

The *Grammar* dialog box offers a few additional options for the *Word* user. If you click on **Grammar ...**, you'll see another pop-up window.

 If at any point while reading this book, you would like to learn more about a topic, click on the question mark in the upper right corner of the screen, just above the *Ribbon*. You can explore topics when they interest you, which will help you to learn them.

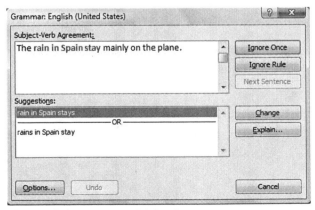

Figure 6-6. *Grammar Dialog Box*

Here are your options for commands in the Grammar dialog box.

- **Ignore Once**. *Word* will ignore this one occurrence of the broken grammar rule.
- **Ignore Rule**. *Word* will ignore all occurrences of this rule being broken in the document.
- **Change**. Will change the underlined text to the text highlighted in the *Suggestions* box.
- **Explain**. *Word* opens a *Help* box that attempts to explain the grammar rule.
- **Options**. Opens the *Proofing* pane in the *Word Options* box.

You might also notice that the word *plane* did not earn a squiggly line. As anyone who might have heard this expression before knows, the rain in Spain is on the *plain*, not the *plane*. That's one more reason to read over your documents after finishing them, even if you've done spell checking with *Word*. We'll leave it to you to purposefully misspell a word and see how you can have *Word* correct it. Simply right click on the misspelled word and select the correct spelling in the dialog box.

Now, let's take a moment to look at the **Look Up ...** command. Right click on the squiggly line and select **Look Up ...**.

Figure 6-7. *Look Up ... commands*

These commands allow you to search *Encarta* and go online for various searches. Clicking on **Research Options ...** will open a dialog box that allows you to select online sites that will appear in the **Look Up ...** commands.

Autocorrect

Word 2007 corrects some mistakes automatically as you type. For example, some people might have the **shift** button depressed too long when capitalizing the first word in a sentence. This would cause the second letter in the word to also be capitalized. *Word 2010* recognizes this as a common error and automatically corrects it by changing the second letter to lower case.

To open the *Autocorrect* dialog box:

1. Open a new document.
2. Click on the **Microsoft Office** button to go to the *Backstage* view.
3. Select the **Word Options** button near the bottom of the pane.
4. A dialog pane opens. Select **Proofing** in the left menu column.
5. Click on **AutoCorrect Options ...** button
6. The *AutoCorrect* dialog box opens.

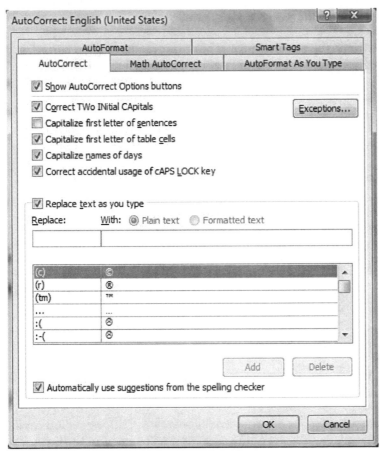

Figure 6-8. *Autocorrect Dialog Box*

You can see five different tabs in the *AutoCorrect* dialog box. The *AutoCorrect* tab is the default tab. Here you can checkboxes that direct *Word* to correct items as they are typed. We've already talked about the first two letters of a word being capitalized, a correction rule identified in the second checkbox.

But what if you were writing about identification cards and wanted to shorten it to IDs? The first two letters in IDs are capitalized. This is called an exception. If you click on the **Exceptions** button, you'll see *ID* is an exception to the rule. You can enter other exceptions to the rule from here.

As you can see in the *AutoCorrect* dialog box, *Word* will capitalize days of the week automatically if you forget. It also corrects for accidentally setting the **caps lock** key.

Word will also capitalize the first words in the cells of a table. We'll talk about tables later.

 If you're taking notes (we encourage writing in the margins of this book!), you can make a note about the capitalizing of words in tables, and when tables are explained, you'll be ahead of the game.

At the bottom, you can see that *Word* will insert frown faces with you type a certain sequence of letters and characters. Use the scroll bar to see what other icons and symbols *Word* will automatically change when it sees those specific combinations.

We're not going to worry about the *Math AutoCorrect* and the *SmartTags* tabs in this book, but you can type those subjects into *Word Help* if you want to read about them.

For now, let's move on to the *AutoFormat* tabs.

AutoFormat

Click on the *AutoFormat* tab to take a look at the *AutoFormat* dialog box.

Figure 6-9. *Autoformat Dialog Box*

As you can see, some of these formatting commands cover areas that this book hasn't yet delved into. That's ok. We'll talk about styles and bulleted lists later.

For now, let's look at the four most important features on this pane and what they do.

- **"Straight quotes" with "smart quotes"** Straight quotes are used for denoting inches. Note that if you want straight quotes, simply click on **Undo** after *Word* performs the automatic formatting function.
- **Ordinals (1st) with superscript** When you type 1st, *Word* will replace it with 1st.
- **Fractions (1/2) with fraction character (½)** When you type 1/2, *Word* will replace it with ½.
- **Hyphens (--) with dash (—)** Type two dashes in a row and *Word* will replace it with a dash.

Now let's look at the *AutoFormat As You Type* tab.
AutoFormat As You Type

Click on the AutoFormat tab to take a look at the AutoFormat dialog box.

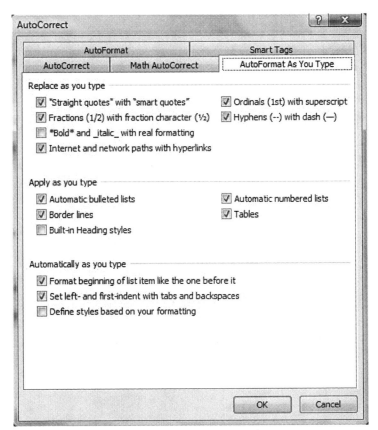

Figure 6-10. *AutoFormat As You Type Dialog Box*

We've already talked about many of these checkbox rules. The difference here is that these automatic formatting changes will occur as you type.

If you have *AutoFormat as you type* turned off, you can still automatically format a document. To do that, we're going to add the **AutoFormat Now** command to the *Quick Access Toolbar*, which is the toolbar beside the **Microsoft Office** button.

Adding Command to Quick Access Toolbar

These are the steps to add the **AutoFormat Now** command to the *Quick Access Toolbar*. When you have time, look through the other commands that you can add. If you find a command that you use often, these are the steps to adding the command. They're the same steps to add any command.

1. Open a new document.
2. Click on the **Customize Quick Access Toolbar** button, which is the rightmost command on the *Quick Access Toolbar*.
3. Select **More Commands ...**
4. Select **All Commands** from the *Choose commands from* drop-down menu.
5. A list of commands appears for you to select from. Scroll down by using the side scroll bar to find **AutoFormat Now**.

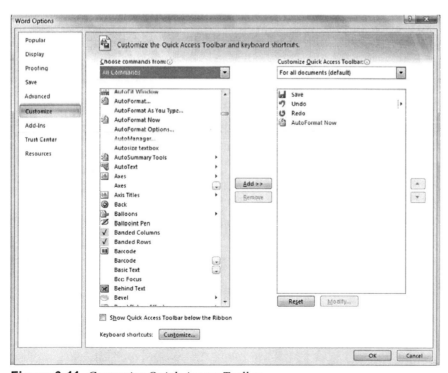

Figure 6-11. *Customize Quick Access Toolbar*

Customize Quick Access Toolbar

1. Select **AutoFormat Now**.
2. Click on the **Add >>** command button.
3. Click **OK**.

You now have the **AutoFormat Now** command on your *Quick Access Toolbar*. If you have automatic formatting turned off, click on the **AutoFormat Now** command button in your *Quick Access Toolbar* to apply the formatting rules you've selected in this chapter.

Review

Let's say you've typed some test and want to send it out for review. It could be that you're sending an essay to an editor or a technical document to engineers for specification checks. Regardless of the reason, you might want to turn on **Track Changes** so you can see what changes are made and who has made them.

We've typed some sample text into a document and have turned on Track Changes. Here's what our screen looks like.

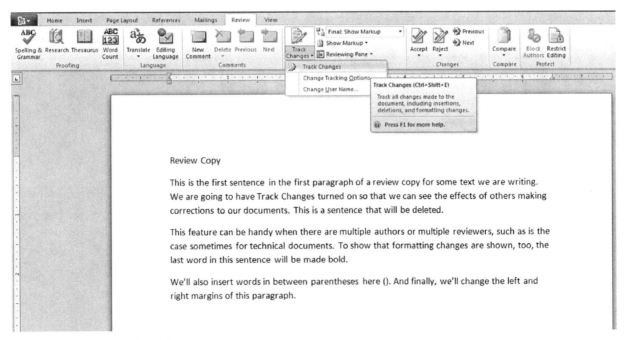

Figure 6-12. *Review Copy Text*

If you read our *Review Copy*, you can see that we've prompted our "reviewers" to make certain changes, namely, to delete the last sentence in the first paragraph, to make a word bold in the second paragraph, and to insert words and change the margins in the third paragraph.

So, we send our document to our reviewer, (RH, or Robin Hewitt, a co-author of this book) and the document comes back with the changes highlighted in various ways, underlining, different color of text, and strikethrough text.

You can select options in **Reviewing Pane, Show Markup**, and **Final Show Markup** to change the way your edited document appears. These commands are in the *Tracking* group in the *Review* Ribbon. You can also select **Accept** or **Reject** in the *Changes* group to accept or reject changes as you place your cursor in each change. Select **Previous** and **Next** to go to the next or previous change made in your document.

You can also **Restrict Editing** in the *Protect* group and **Compare** the edited document to an earlier saved version of the document in the *Compare* group.

In the *Comments* group, you can add comments by selecting **New Comment**. You might want to add a comment to the document that is addressed to the person who is going to be reviewing your document. You can make it personal if you know the person, but remember that it's a permanent record. You can also delete comments or move to the next or previous comment.

The *Language* group allows you to make translations of your document and to select the language for translation.

The *Proofing* group allows you to count the words in your document, to look up synonyms of a word in the **Thesaurus**, and to **Research** words or topics online in Encarta or other online sources.

Let's take a look at what our edited document, our Review Copy, looks like when we get it back from our reviewer.

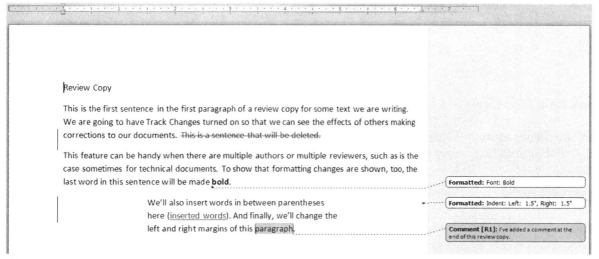

Figure 6-13. *Edited Review Copy Test*

As you can see, the editor (note the comment "*R1*" is an identifier) has made the changes in the document. If there were multiple people making edits, each editor's comments would be in a different color and have a different identifier.

We'll click on each change, either in the text or in the balloon in the right margin, and then with the change highlighted, we'll click on **Accept Change**. As you accept a change, the next change becomes highlighted.

Note you can also select **Accept** and then select **Accept All Changes** to accept all of the changes made to your document.

Here's what our document looks like after we've accepted all of the changes. Note that the comment will still show on your screen but will not print. You can view what your printed document will look like if you select **Final: Show Markup** and then select **Final**.

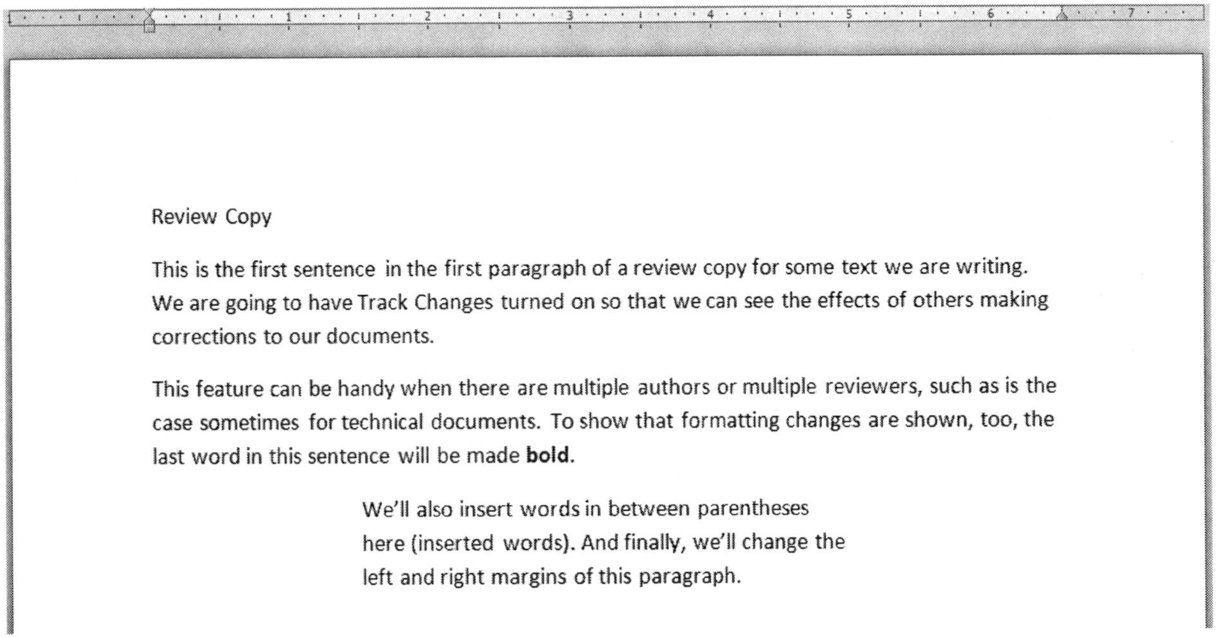

Review Copy

This is the first sentence in the first paragraph of a review copy for some text we are writing. We are going to have Track Changes turned on so that we can see the effects of others making corrections to our documents.

This feature can be handy when there are multiple authors or multiple reviewers, such as is the case sometimes for technical documents. To show that formatting changes are shown, too, the last word in this sentence will be made **bold**.

We'll also insert words in between parentheses here (inserted words). And finally, we'll change the left and right margins of this paragraph.

Figure 6-14. *Final Copy*

There are plenty of ways to change the appearance of edits made to your document. You can change the color of altered text, select the changes to appear as balloons in the right margin, and so on.

Summary

In this chapter, we've shown how you can perform spell checking and grammar checking on your documents. You can do this as you type, or you can wait until you're finished with the document, then go back and perform the functions. You can also perform formatting features in the same way.

We've shown you a great way to customize your *Quick Access Toolbar*, making command buttons that you use frequently available no matter which tab you're working with and which commands are shown in the *Ribbon*.

We've also shown you how to use some of the new Review features of Word 2010. You can visually see the changes to your document with colors and balloons.

There are also translation commands, research commands, and compare and protect commands. Explore these features by using Word Help as needed.

By using the features in this chapter, you can go a long way in making your documents more professional, and you just might learn a little about spelling and grammar along the way.

Chapter 7

■ ■ ■

Techniques for Headers and Footers

Introduction

After the last chapter with spelling and grammar checking, you should be starting to feel comfortable that your *Word 2010* documents have words that are correctly spelled and your sentences are properly constructed.

In this chapter, we're going to go over headers and footers. These two terms are aptly named. Just as the head is at the top of the body, the header is at the top of the page. And of course the foot and footer are at the bottom of the body and page respectively.

If you have ever read a novel, you'll notice that the title of the book (sometimes) and the page number are at the top or bottom of each page. These are headers or footers. Sometimes the author name and chapter title are included.

Why bother with headers and footers at all?

Headers and footers help readers know where they're at in a document. The location can be identified by page number, section number, or chapter. Also, page numbering is automated, saving time.

Imagine the old days when page numbers had to be inserted manually!

In a classroom chemistry report, for example, you could have a header that breaks the report down into *Procedure* and *Results*, for example.

Imagine a teacher or instructor who is grading your report and begins to carry it to another room. But the dog gets in the way and trips the teacher. The pages of your report scatter like newspapers blown away in gust of wind. If you have headers that number the pages of your report, it can easily be put back in order (providing the dog doesn't eat any of it).

Insert a Header

Let's open a new document and place a header in it. We're going to write a report about a book we have read. It's an imaginary book we're calling *The Romans Spoke Latin But It's All Greek to Me.* To give a document a header:

1) Open a new document.
2) Position the pointer at the top of the page.
3) Double click.
4) The *Header & Footer Design Ribbon* opens.

Notice that the *Ribbon* is populated by new *Groups*. Also, a new *Tab* has appeared. The new *Tab* is titled *Design*. The groups in this *Ribbon* are associated with the *Header & Footer Design* tab.

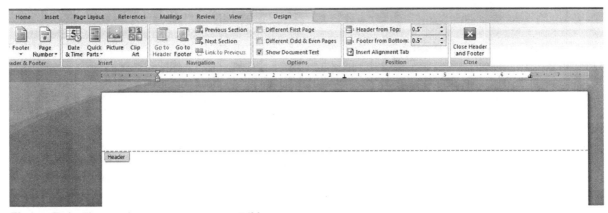

Figure 7-1. *The Header & Footer Design Ribbon*

Now, let's put the title of our book report into the header. Type the name. You might have to click your pointer in the header area (above the dashed line) to move your insertion point to the header, but it should be there when you open the *Header & Footer Ribbon*.

Figure 7-2. *Document Title as Header Text*

Notice that we have italicized our title. You can select the text, and then go to the *Home* tab and select **Italics** or de-select it depending on your preferences. You could also select the text and pick **Italics** from the mini-Toolbar.

Also notice that the ruler is shown. You can position the text in the *Header* in the same way that text in the document is positioned via *Ruler* settings.

Positioning and Page Numbering

We want our header to be centered on each page of our report.

1) Select the text in the header.
2) Go to the *Home* tab.
3) Select **Center** in the *Paragraph* group.

The Romans Spoke Latin But It's All Greek to Me

Figure 7-3. *Centered Header Text*

Note that the text is still highlighted. You have to click your pointer somewhere in the active writing area (in this case, somewhere in the *Header*) to de-select the text.

Microsoft Word 2010 is like other *Word* applications. When text is selected and an operation is performed on the selected text, the text will stay selected until you de-select the text.

Now let's add a page number. Some people prefer simply to have the page number on the header. Other people like to type "page" then add a space and the number. Still other people like to type "p." and then have the number. Choose whichever appeals to you most.

4) To add the page number:
5) Click at the end of the header text.
6) Tap the spacebar twice.
7) Type "page".
8) Tap the spacebar once.
9) Select the *Insert* tab. (Optional.)
10) Find the *Header & Footer* group. Note: this group also appears on the *Design* tab.

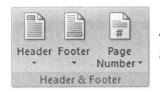

This is the *Header & Footer* group. Note that **Page Number** has an arrowhead to open a list of commands.

> 11) Click on **Page Number** in the *Header & Footer* group.

You'll see that you have some choices of commands. These commands prompt you to select where you want to put the page number.

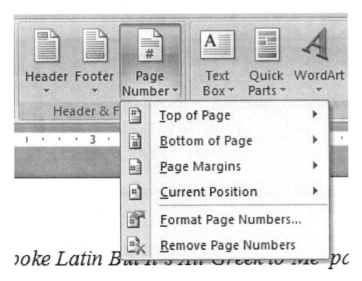

Figure 7-4. *Page Number Commands*

We've already positioned our cursor where we want to put the page number, so …:

> 12) Select **Current Position**.

You'll see that *Word* gives you more choices. And not only that, *Word 2010* gives you examples of what your document will look like with each command choice. These types of examples are provided for different selections under the **Page Number** command.

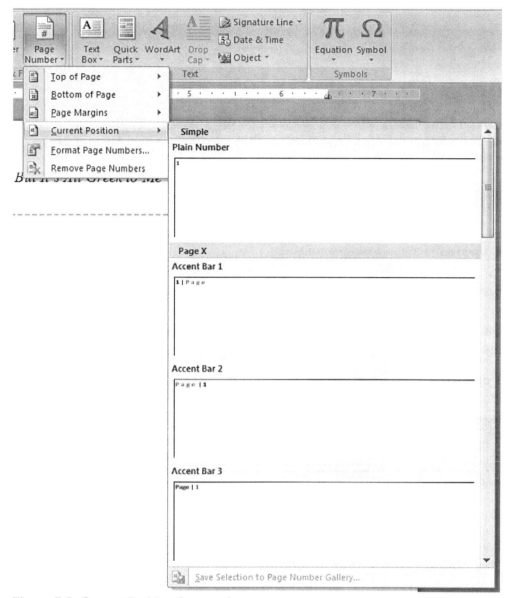

Figure 7-5. *Current Position Commands*

We're not going to worry about the *Accent Bars*. If you want to play with those, select them. For now, we're going with a beginner's choice.

     13) Select **Plain Number**.
     14) Select the *Design* tab if you're currently under the *Insert* tab.
     15) Click on **Close Header and Footer**.

Congratulations! You now have a page number and the title of your report at the top of your page. When you type your report, the header will appear at the top of each page. The page number will increment and show the actual number of the page.

Page Numbers

You don't have to type text into a header when you just want the page number. Simply go to the *Insert* tab and find the *Header & Footer* group. Select **Page Number**, then select the position for your page number. Some of the options will have "Page" already in it, so *Word 2010* does it for you.

Different First Page

You may have noticed a command called **Format Page Number ...** when you clicked on the **Page Number** command to open a list of numbering commands.

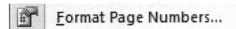   This is the **Format Page Numbers ...** command.

Go back to your book report and open the header. Click on **Page Number** and then click on **Format Page Numbers ...**. You'll see another set of commands.

These commands not only allow you to select the text formatting characteristics of your page numbers, you have some options for where to start your numbering from.

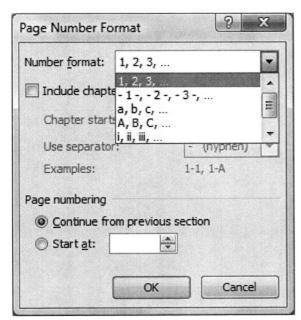

Figure 7-6. *Page Number Format*

In this box, you can select the kind of numbering you want. You could "number" your pages with successive letters or Roman numerals. You can also click on the **Start at:** option and start you page numbering at a number other than 1. This is useful if you're working on several sections of a report, and each section has its own *Word* file. You can start numbering the second section with the page number after the last page number of the first section.

Footers

We're going to make this simple. The only difference between the *Footer* commands and the *Header* commands is the position on the page. Everything we're showing you in the *Header* also applies to the *Footer*. If you want your report title and page numbers at the bottom of the page, you simple repeat the steps except double clicking at the bottom of the page to open the *Header & Footer Design* tab and begin editing in the footer area (bottom) of the page.

Note that you can also access the *Header & Footer Design Ribbon* from the *Insert* tab and selecting the **Header** or **Footer** command. Try each method and see which one feels more comfortable for you. Also note that if you already have a header or footer in your document, this is where you select the command to edit them.

Header & Footer Design

The *Header & Footer Design* tab, as we've pointed out, opens a new *Ribbon* with new groups. Let's take a look at these groups and see what the commands do.

Here's a closer look at the *Header & Footer Design* ribbon.

Figure 7-7. *Header & Footer Design Ribbon*

The first group is the *Header & Footer* group.

Header & Footer Group

Part of the reason we're writing this book is to help *Word 2010* users become familiar with *Word* commands, with the *Word* interface on the computer monitor, and to help you become more comfortable and confident that you can accomplish whatever you want with the appearance of your documents.

To that end, we might have repeat pictures of groups in several places in this book. That's okay. We want you to become more familiar with the appearance of these groups.

Figure 7-8. *Header & Footer Group*

We've already talked about these commands, but we'll summarize them here.

 Header This command allows you to select from several *header* templates. It also has the **Remove Header** and **Edit Header** commands.

 Footer This command allows you to select from several *footer* templates. It also has the **Remove Footer** and **Edit Footer** commands.

 Page Number This command gives you options of where to insert the page number. It also has the **Format Page Numbers ...** and **Remove Page Numbers** commands.

Insert Group

This group allows you to insert various items into the header.

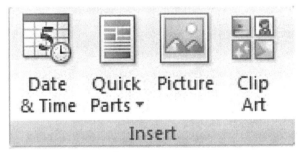

Figure 7-9. *Insert Group*

Here's a breakdown of each command.

Date
& Time

Date & Time This inserts the data and/or time and allows you to choose the format.

Quick
Parts ▾

Quick Parts This commands allows you to insert document properties.

Picture

Picture This allows you to insert a picture previously saved as a file. We'll cover inserting pictures in a later chapter.

Clip
Art

Clip Art This allows you to insert clip art, which are pictures, too, only not taken with a camera. They're picture art that *Word* has ready for you to use.

Navigation Group

Want to move around from header to footer, from one page to the next while editing headers and footers? The *Navigation* group is the place to be!

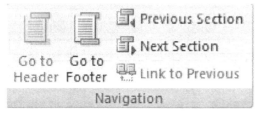

Figure 7-10. *Navigation Group*

Here's a summary of the commands in the *Navigation* group.

Go to
Header

Go to Header This switches you to the header to edit it if you're editing the footer. The command is grayed out if you're already working in the header.

Go to
Footer

Go to Footer This switches you from editing the header to the footer.

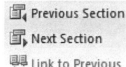 **Section Commands** When you insert section breaks, you can move to headers (and footers) associated with a previous or with the next section. This is useful if you're writing a novel and you want the chapter number in the header. Simply create section breaks and different headers for the specific sections.

Options Group

The *Options* group gives you some choices for setting up your headers and footers.

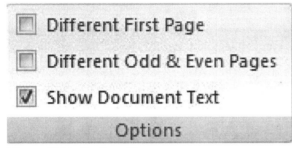

Figure 7-11. *Options Group*

These are options that allow you to set up numbering for projects that have page numbering issues, such as a title page in which there would be no page number shown because it is obviously the first page.

Let's look at each of these optional commands in the *Options* group.

Different First Page This allows you to have a different header on the first page. This is useful if you have a report and don't want a header on the first (title) page. Just have a different first page and leave the first page header blank.

Different Odd & Even Pages This lets you have different headers on odd and even pages. If you're going to bind a book, the odd and even pages will have headers that will differ because they'll be aligned with the right and left margins.

Show Document Text This checkbox shows or hides the document text when you're editing the header or footer.

Position Group

Commands in the *Position* group place your headers and footers where you want them.

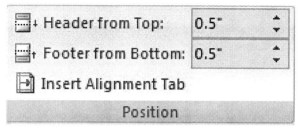

Figure 7-12. *Position Group*

With the commands in this group, you can position you headers and footers, say, a half inch from the edge of the page. That's the default distance, but you can change it if you want.

 Some printers cannot printer closer than a set distance from the edge of the paper. If you're printing documents, make sure your headers and footers will print. If not, move them farther from the edge of the paper.

Let's take a look at the commands in the *Position* group.

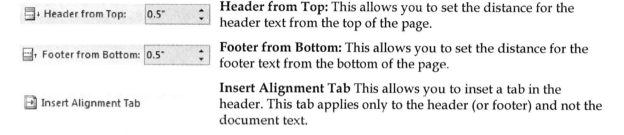

Header from Top: This allows you to set the distance for the header text from the top of the page.

Footer from Bottom: This allows you to set the distance for the footer text from the bottom of the page.

Insert Alignment Tab This allows you to inset a tab in the header. This tab applies only to the header (or footer) and not the document text.

Close Group

There's only one command in this group, so it's hardly worth calling a group, but that's the way the *Headers & Footers Design* ribbon comes to us, and we're just the messengers here.

Figure 7-13. *Close Group*

This command closes the *Headers & Footers Design* ribbon. The headers and footers editing areas will close. That is, they will become grayed out so that they can no longer be edited, until, that is, you open the *Headers & Footers Design* ribbon again.

 If you make a mistake, click on **Undo**. It works just the same when you're editing headers and footers.

Summary

In this chapter, we've shown you how to work with headers and footers. This could be a class formatting requirement for term papers. Many teachers want your name on each page, especially if it's a printed report. It is a great way to mark your stamp on every printed page. You can put your name in the header, and it will be printed.

We've also shown how you can insert page numbering into your document. The page numbering can be in a variety of formats and located in different areas of each page. Putting the page number in the header is a great organizational tool.

Reports and class assignments typically have a first page that could be considered a title page. The title page might have the student's name and class name. It might have the semester and year listed. You wouldn't want the header to show that it's page 1 because it's obviously the first page. So we've shown you how to locate the **Different First Page** checkbox.

We've shown you the commands in the *Headers & Footers Design* ribbon. If headers and footers are important to you, take the time to explore the different commands and how they affect the appearance of your headers and footers.

Chapter 8

■ ■ ■

Insert Techniques

Introduction

The *Insert* tab brings with it a powerful ribbon. With it, you can insert all sorts of wonderful things into your document. We're going to cover some of these options in later chapters. For example, we'll devote an entire chapter to tables, which can be inserted with the **Table** command under the *Insert* tab.

For now, we want to keep our outlook that this is a book for people who want to have a basic understanding of *Word 2010*, and we're going to cover the *Illustrations* group under the *Insert* tab, along with a few new features of *Word 2010*. To start with, we'll show you how to insert pictures. We'll also insert a text box and a screenshot.

The **Insert Screenshot** command is a new command for *Word 2010*, and it can come in handy when you see something on your computer screen that you want to capture, perhaps to show to someone else later. Simply capture the screenshot, insert it into a *Word* document, then save the document. You could also add some descriptive text.

The pictures that you insert can be in the form of a file that you saved from your camera, or they can be clipart, which are drawings and pictures that come with *Word*.

We will also be showing how to insert a text box. Text boxes are great ways to associate text with a picture. You can insert other things, too, like arrows. Then you can arrange the arrows to point at objects in your picture, such as a test tube in a chemistry lab or a spot on the beach where you went swimming last year.

We'll also show you a few formatting commands to help you get a fast start on making the most of your inserted pictures.

Insert a Picture

We're going to assume you know at this stage how to open a file, so we're going to start abbreviating some of our step-by-step instructions. But don't worry; we won't jump too far ahead.

In our instructions, we'll be asking you to type some text. This is so that you'll know how the text is affected by the picture you insert. The picture or clipart you're going to insert will be inserted at the insertion point. You'll be able to move the picture or clipart after insertion, but it's always helpful to know ahead of time where the picture will appear.

It might be helpful at this point for you to think about how you'll be using *Word*. If you're going to write family update letters, write a practice letter when a step says to type some text. If you're writing reports for school, type in an imaginary report. The more practice you get, the better you'll become with *Word*.

So let's get started.

    1) Open a new document.
    2) Type some text, say two or three paragraphs.
    3) Click on the *Insert* tab.
    4) Find the *Illustrations* group. We're going to cover the various commands in the *Illustrations* group later in this chapter. For now, we want you to see where we're working.

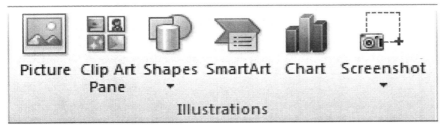

Figure 8-1. *The Illustrations Group*

    5) Click on Picture.

The *Insert Picture* dialog box appears. We've selected the *Sample Pictures* location.

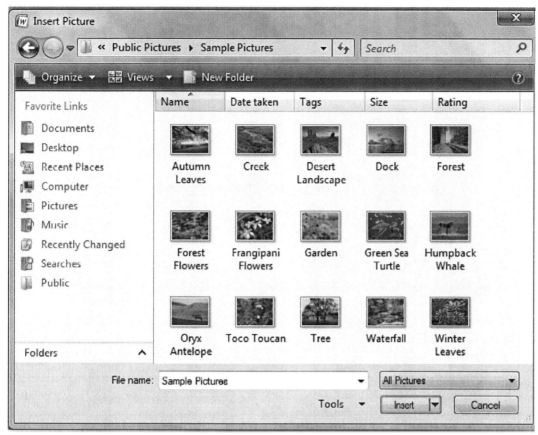

Figure 8-2. *The Insert Picture Dialog Box*

This is how to insert a picture from a file. Find your file from your *Desktop*, from your *Documents* folder, or from wherever you have them stored. If you have them on a flash drive, you can click on *Computer* and find your flash drive there.

For now, let's pretend we're going to change our mind, now that we have the *Insert Picture* dialog box open. We'll cancel out of this box and go to the **Clip Art** command.

> 6) Click on Cancel in the Insert Picture dialog box.
> 7) Select Clip Art.
> 8) The Clip Art pane opens.

Figure 8-3. *The Clip Art Pane*

We're not going to go into depth on explaining what you can do with the *Clip Art* pane, which appears on the right side of the *Word* display, but we want to point out a few options in this pane. First, here's what we're planning to do. We'll scroll down the list of pictures (clipart figures) and select one with our pointer. The picture will appear in our document at our insertion point. Our insertion point will be at the bottom of our text, as we don't want the picture interfering with our text layout. Besides, we haven't decided yet where to place the picture.

What other actions could you do from the Clip Art pane?

- **Search for:** Search your computer or selected folders for clip art with a specific file name.
- **Search in:** You can organize your clip art in separate collection locations.
- **Results should be:** You can select photographs, movies, sounds, and clipart.
- **Organize clips ...** Opens an organizer pane so you can see the file locations.
- **Clip art on Office Online** Go online and search the Microsoft collection of clipart.
- **Tips for finding clips** A help button for help specific to clipart.
- **X button** It's in the upper right corner of the pane. You'll need to select **X** to exit the pane.

Now, let's get back to our assignment. Remember, we've typed our text into a new document, and now we're going to insert a picture.

9) Use the scroll bar to find the picture you want.
10) Click on the picture.
11) Click on the X to exit the Clip Art pane.

Here's how our assignment looks at this point.

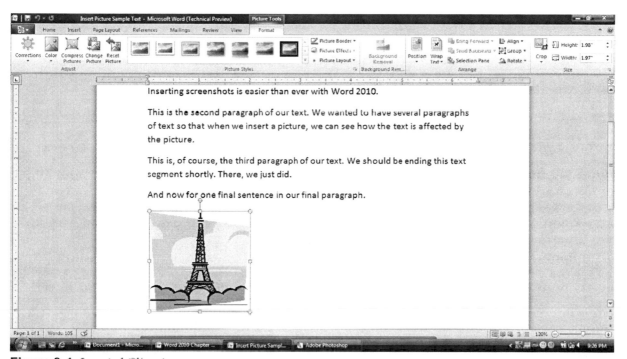

Figure 8-4. *Inserted Clipart*

We want to point out a few things before moving on.

Note that this clipart picture is still selected.

Just like text that has been selected and moved (or has had some operation performed on it), the picture will stay selected until you deselect it by clicking your pointer somewhere else in the document.

Also note the small circles at the corners and sides of the picture. These are *handles*. If you move your pointer over a handle, press the left mouse button down, and drag your pointer while continuing to keep the button pressed down, you can manually change the size of your picture.

The small circle above the picture allows you to rotate the picture via the same, press-button-and-drag method.

Also, the ribbon has changed. Because you have inserted a picture, *Word* automatically switches the ribbon to the *Format Ribbon* for a new *Picture Tools* tab. We'll use a few of the commands in this *Format Ribbon* to reposition our picture.

For now, let's just deselect the picture.

The Picture Tools Format Ribbon

When you deselect the picture, you might lose the *Picture Tools Format* ribbon, which is what we want to talk about. So how do you get the ribbon back? Click on the picture and select the *Picture Tools Format* tab.

Okay. Now that you have the ribbon back in view, let's take a look at it.

Figure 8-5. *The Picture Tools Format Ribbon*

In the middle part of the ribbon, you'll see some different frames and effects that you can apply to your picture. These are in the *Picture Styles* group. We won't go over each one, but you could select a nice frame for your picture.

Let's take a moment to look at some of the other groups. We're going to position our picture manually, and we're going to set the size by dragging a handle, but if you wanted to do things differently you could use this ribbon to accomplish the same effects.

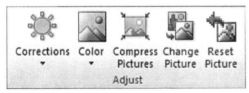

Corrections Opens a menu that allows you to change the contrast and brightness of the picture. You can also change picture sharpness.

Color Opens a palette of choices. Select color saturation, color tone, or recolor the picture with different hues. You can also change picture color options here, as well as set a color as transparent.

Compress Pictures Reduces the file size of the picture (useful for large files).

Change Picture Swaps the selected picture with another one that you get to select.

Reset Picture Removes changes you've made to the picture.

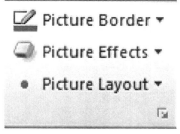

Picture Border Select border color and style.
Picture Effects Choose an effect such as a shadow, glow, reflection or 3-D rotation for your picture.
Picture Layout Choose a predetermined layout that changes shape of picture and adds text.

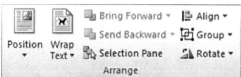

Position Select picture placement on page.
Wrap Text Select the way text appears when it is near your picture.
Selection Pane Allows you to select objects on the page and layer them.
Align Choose from a variety of alignment options for your picture such as centered.
Group Make several pictures combine into one object you can perform operations on.
Rotate Choose from different rotation commands, including upside down.

Crop Cut off sections of the picture. Select this command, then move the picture handles to cut.
Height, Width: Manually select the size of your picture.
Arrow Launcher Opens *Size* dialog box with additional commands.

Adjust Commands

The palette of choices that *Word 2010* gives you when you adjust your pictures adjust many of the same characteristics as earlier versions of *Word*. But *Word 2010* shows you what the changes will look like. Let's take a momentary sidetrack from inserting a picture from **Clip Art**.

We'll insert a picture into a blank *Word* document and show you what the command choices look like. First, let's look at the **Corrections** command.

Figure 8-6. *The Corrections Command Palette*

As you move your pointer over the palette of choices, the effects will appear in a text box. In our example, we adjusted the brightness and contrast by 20 percent. You can also select Picture Correction Options to manually select brightness and contrast settings.

Now let's look at the **Color** command.

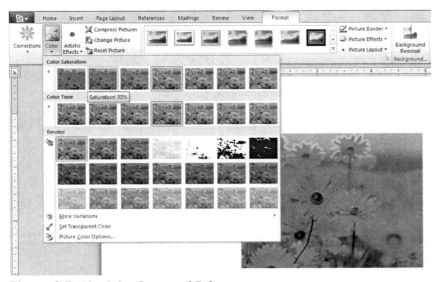

Figure 8-7. *The Color Command Palette*

Move your pointer over each picture example to see what the effect will be on your picture. In our example, we changed the color saturation to 33 percent. Note the **Picture Color Options ...** command. Use this command to enter changes manually.

Now let's look at what the **Artistic Effects** command can do for your picture. Select you picture then click on **Artistic Effects**.

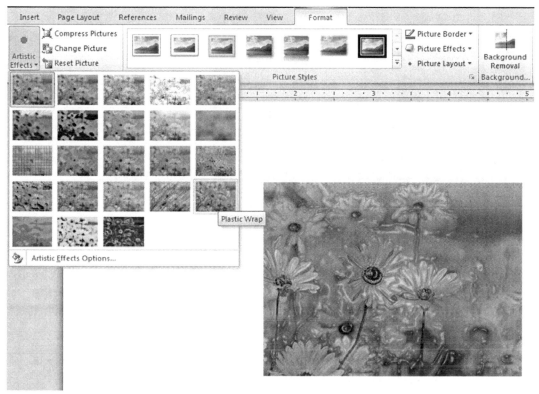

Figure 8-8. *The Artistic Effects Command Palette*

These artistic commands allow you to have different effects for your pictures. Note you can also select more options with **Artistic Effects Options ....**

New Word 2010 Picture Techniques

Before we move on, we simply must cover two of the new commands available in *Word 2010* that pertain to pictures.

These commands are on the *Format* ribbon.

Let's look at a new picture for these commands. If you want to practice these commands, insert a picture of a turtle from your *Sample Pictures* subfolder in your *Pictures* folder.

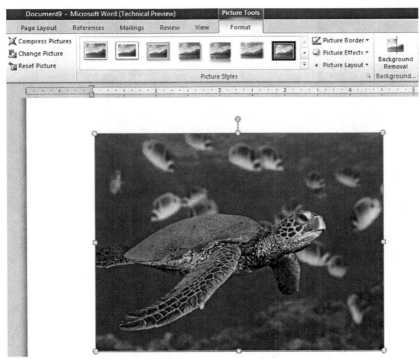

Figure 8-9. *Inserted Turtle Picture*

Now select **Background Removal.** You'll be presented with a layout that allows you to choose the object in your picture from which you want the background removed. Use the picture handles to move the highlighted foreground item.

You also have mark to include and delete commands.

Figure 8-10. *Background Removal Screen*

Click on **Close Background Removal** to finalize your choice.

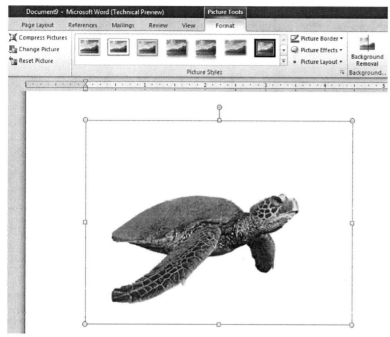

Figure 8-11. *Background Removed*

There is another new feature that is available on the Picture Format ribbon.
It's the **Picture Layout** command. Click on it to see what your choices look like.

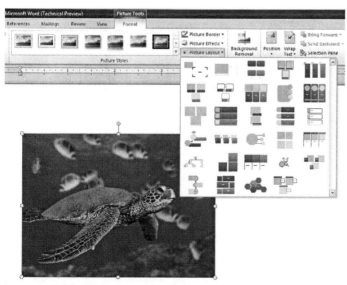

Figure 8-12. *Picture Layout Command Menu*

Move your pointer over the diagram layouts in the menu and the picture will change to show how your selection of commands would appear on the page.

Figure 8-13. *Picture Layout Circle Choice*

When you select a choice on the menu, a screen will appear that allows you to enter your caption choice. Here is our final result.

Figure 8-14. *Turtle Picture with Text*

Now, there's one more *Word 2010* technique that needs discussion on the *Insert* Ribbon. It's called the **Screenshot** command. We've added a text box to our turtle picture (we'll cover that later) and then selected **Print Screen** from the keyboard. This key is sometimes shorted to **Prnt Scrn**, probably to fit onto the key.

Remember, **Screenshots** is an insertion command. It is in the *Illustrations* group under the *Insert* tab. When you select it, you'll see a picture of the screen that was visible when you pressed **Prnt Scrn**. Click on it. There may be other selections available from your clipboard.

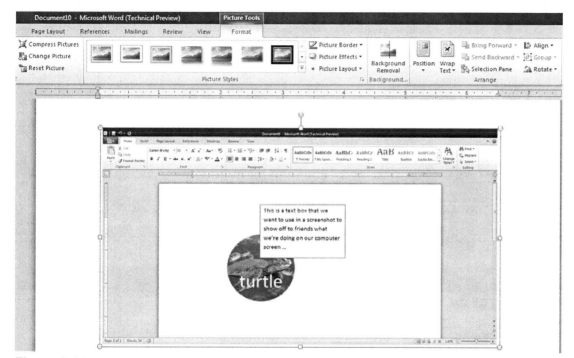

Figure 8-15. *Inserted Screenshot*

Some possible applications for inserting screenshots include directions for following a procedure that you are doing on your computer. Let's say you know how to select text, insert a picture, and loop up a map on the Internet. As you perform steps, select **Prnt Scrn**. Then you can later insert your screenshots into a document and add text to describe what you're doing. Save the document and send it along to describe your computer actions.

Another possible application is the appearance of an error message or a log file. Simply use **Prnt Scrn** and you can send a replication of the message as it appears on your screen to anyone!

You can also use it for online applications. If you are entering data into a form on a website, you can use **Prnt Scrn** for a record of the data you entered.

Picture Commands

Let's go back to our inserted clip art of the Eiffel Tower. It's easy to get sidetracked with all of the new functionality of *Word 2010*, so we're going to show you the file we were working with. Save your files so that if you're interrupted, you can open them later and continue following along.

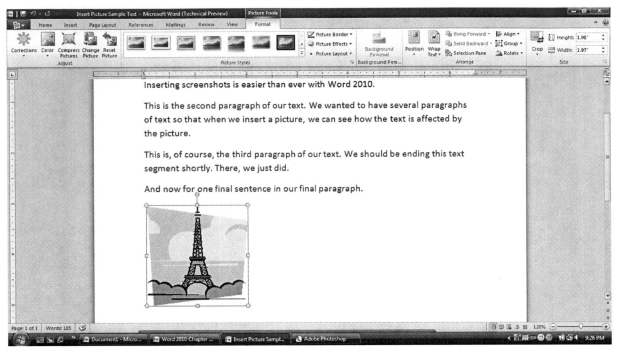

Figure 8-16. *Inserted Clip Art*

We're going to perform some commands on our picture and hopefully present ideas on what to do with yours. First, we're going to move our picture up and have the text nestled up nicely right beside it. We do this with a feature called text wrapping.

1) Select your picture.
2) Select **Text Wrapping** in the *Arrange* group.
3) Select **Tight**. (Note your other options for your later personal use.)
4) Click on the picture.
5) With your pointer over the picture, depress the left mouse button.
6) Keep the mouse button depressed and drag your picture up.
7) Release the mouse button.

You should have a document that now has a picture with text wrapped around it. See how ours looks. You can drag the picture higher or lower per your preferences.

This is some text we are typing for Chapter 8 of Learning New Techniques with Microsoft Word 2010. We will be inserting a picture, a text box, and a screenshot. Inserting screenshots is easier than ever with Word 2010.

This is the second paragraph of our text. We wanted to have several paragraphs of text so that when we insert a picture, we can see how the text is affected by the picture.

This is, of course, the third paragraph of our text. We should be ending this text segment shortly. There, we just did.

And now for one final sentence in our final paragraph.

Figure 8-17. *Text Wrapping Around Picture*

What you want to keep in mind here is that you have other options for how the picture is aligned with the page and with the text. You can align it with the right side of the page, center it, make it bigger, put a frame around it, and change the coloring.

 Now is a good time to look at some of the other text wrapping options. Select the picture, then select the **Text Wrapping** command. Select another text wrapping option, such as **In Line with Text**. Look at how it affects your document. Click **Undo** to change back. Move the picture around within the text and see the results. This is a valuable strategy to learn how *Word* commands affect the appearance of your document.

All of the alignment commands are available for you on the *Picture Tools Format* ribbon. Just keep in mind that you will need to have your picture selected when you perform an operation on it.

You'll know the picture is selected because it will have the handles (small circles) surrounding it in the borders.

So now, let's add a text box to identify our picture.

Add Text Box

There are about a zillion things you can do with text boxes. Other books will go into great detail about those commands. We're going to sidestep most of them.

Keep in mind that a text box is exactly what it sounds like, a box on the page that you can fill with text. But the neat thing about text boxes is, you can move them around and change the properties just like you can with pictures.

A good way to think about a text box is that it is an object. A picture is also an object. *Word 2010* places objects on the page and associates spacing and other characteristics to these objects.

To add a text box:

>   1) Click on the *Insert* tab.
>   2) Click on **Text Box** in the *Text* group.
>   3) Select **Simple Text Box**.

If you want to explore some additional options later, select a different style of text box. But for now, you should have a *Word* document with a text box inserted at where you last left your insertion point.

 Know where your insertion point is!

Here is our document with an inserted text box:

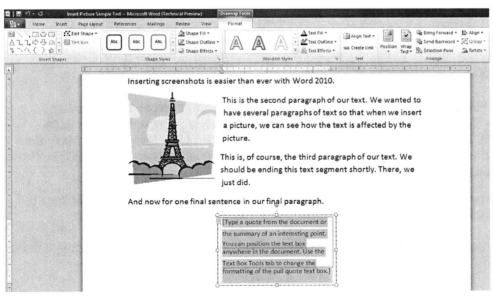

Figure 8-18. *Inserted Text Box*

Note that the text in the text box is already highlighted. You could hit delete and start typing text, or you can simply start typing text (selected text is automatically deleted).

Also note that you have a new ribbon.

This ribbon is called the *Drawing Tools Format* ribbon.

We'll cover some of these commands later, but if you're curious, you can play with them now. They affect how the text appears in the text box, along with other effects.

For now, you've inserted a text box, so we want to show you how to type your text into the text box, re-size the text box, and move the text box where you want it. If you want to explore text box commands, open **Help** and type "text box" into the search box to learn more.

Working with a Text Box

We want to identify our picture as the Eiffel Tower, so with the text selected in your text box (or the text deleted), type "Eiffel Tower". Here's how our text box looks after we type that text.

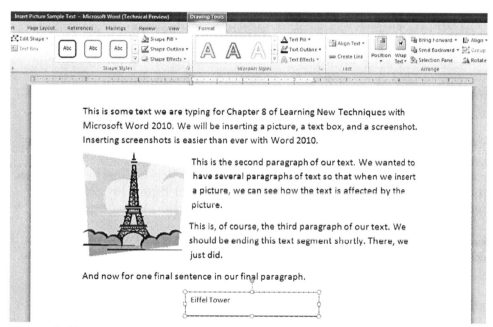

Figure 8-19. *Text Typed Into Text Box*

Note that there are two major problems with our text box.

- The box is much too big for our two simple words.
- The box does not identify the picture because they are not near each other.

In order to correct the size of the text box, remember that a text box is like a picture in that it has "handles." We're going to click on the center handle in the right border of the text box and drag it to the left. Then we'll click on the center handle in the bottom border of the text box and drag it slightly up.

We should now have a nicely sized text box for the text we've typed. You can re-size your text box to whatever size pleases you.

This is, of course, the third paragraph of our text. We should be ending this text segment shortly. There, we just did.

And now for one final sentence in our final paragraph.

Figure 8-20. *Re-sized Text Box*

Now, let's move the text box into the bottom of the picture. Then, visually, it will be an announcement of what the picture is, acting as a label. To move the text box, you have to select it.

 If the text box is too small, part of your text will be hidden. Your text still exists, but you can't see it. Select a text box handle and enlarge the box until all of your text is visible.

There's a common problem with trying to move a text box. You could try to select it by clicking on it, and you could have entered into the text editing mode. This is the mode in which you're typing text into the box. If you click and drag while in this mode, you're going to simply select text in the text box. This is the same way to select any other kind of text in your document. You depress the left mouse key, drag the mouse, and text becomes highlighted until you lift up on the left mouse key.

In order to select the text box as an object (a moveable object), you sometimes will have to click elsewhere in the document first, then re-select the text box by clicking your pointer on the border of it. If you click in the middle area, Word thinks you want to work with the text instead of the box.

Usually, it's easiest to click in the space just above the text box, then lower the pointer to the top border, then left click.

Now that the text box is selected, put your pointer on the top border, left click, and move your mouse. Your text box will move with your mouse movements.

Position the text box over the bottom of the picture and release the mouse button.
Here's how our document looks.

This is some text we are typing for Chapter 8 of Learning New Techniques with Microsoft Word 2010. We will be inserting a picture, a text box, and a screenshot. Inserting screenshots is easier than ever with Word 2010.

This is the second paragraph of our text. We wanted to have several paragraphs of text so that when we insert a picture, we can see how the text is affected by the picture.

This is, of course, the third paragraph of our text. We should be ending this text segment shortly. There, we just did.

And now for one final sentence in our final paragraph.

Figure 8-21. *Re-positioned Text Box*

Insert Arrow

Let's have our report be informative. How tall is the top of the Eiffel Tower? We can show the reader by pointing at the top of the tower with an arrow and adding another text box with the height listed.

We're hoping in this chapter to steer you toward opportunities on how to present your information in a visual way. As much as we enjoy writing, a well-positioned picture and arrow can speak volumes, and visual information is often retained better than the written word.

So:

> 1) Position your insertion point at the bottom of your document.
> 2) Select the *Insert* tab.
> 3) Click on **Shapes**.
> 4) Select the **Line** with a single arrowhead.

You can, of course, select any shape you want. It's easy to get overwhelmed, though. We have found that often the simple choice is the best choice. So what not select a simple arrow to point at what you want to highlight?

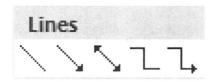

These represent just a few of the selections you can insert from the *Insert* tab, in the *Illustrations* group, with the **Shapes** command. We like the line with a single arrowhead so we can point at what the text is referring to.

To insert the arrow, we're going to click once to start the arrow, then click again to end the arrow.

5) Move your pointer over an area of the document with no text.
6) Click once.
7) Drag your cursor to the right an inch or two.
8) Click again.

Here's what your screen should show after you select a line with an arrowhead.

This is some text we are typing for Chapter 8 of Learning New Techniques with Microsoft Word 2010. We will be inserting a picture, a text box, and a screenshot. Inserting screenshots is easier than ever with Word 2010.

This is the second paragraph of our text. We wanted to have several paragraphs of text so that when we insert a picture, we can see how the text is affected by the picture.

This is, of course, the third paragraph of our text. We should be ending this text segment shortly. There, we just did.

And now for one final sentence in our final paragraph.

Figure 8-22. *Inserted Arrow Shape*

Modifying an AutoShape

Note that the arrow has a small circle at each end. These are the handles, just like a picture has handles. With an arrow, though, we can do a few special tricks. Let's say we want to point the arrow at the top of the Eiffel Tower (not the antenna, though).

First we'll want the arrow to stand out more. Let's make it thicker.

1) Select the arrow by clicking on it.
2) Right click. A command dialog box appears. With these commands, you can cut, copy the object, or connect a hyperlink to the object. With a hyperlink, a URL will need to be typed in. This internet address will be sought out by the default browser when selected. For our purposes, we're going to select **Format Shape**.
3) The *Format Shape* dialog box appears.

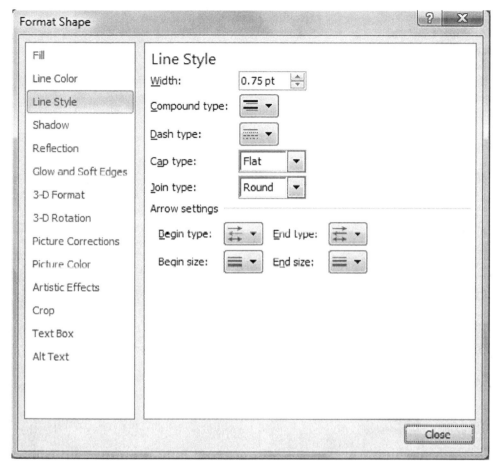

Figure 8-23. *Format Shape Dialog Box*

You'll notice you can change the width of the line, change the line to a compound (double or more) line, make the line a dashed line, and make other changes to how the arrow appears. On the left pane, you can access other change commands, including color commands and 3-D commands. These commands are similar to other inserted object commands.

With each different object, you'll have similar but different options when you select the object and right click, bringing up the autoshape's format dialog box.

Let's go with a 2 pt. weight and a black color for the arrow.

> 4) Select 2 pt in the weight: command.
> 5) Select black color in the Line Color command.
> 6) Now let's move the arrowhead so that it points at the top of the tower.
> 7) Place your pointer over the handle at the arrowhead.
> 8) Depress the left mouse button.

9) Keeping the button pressed, drag the arrowhead to the top of the tower.
10) Release the mouse button.
11) Move your pointer over the handle at the other end of the arrow.
12) Press the left mouse button.
13) Keeping the button pressed, drag the end of the arrow up into the picture, about halfway from the bottom and near the right side of the picture. (We have a reason.)
14) Release the mouse button.

Your picture should now look like this.

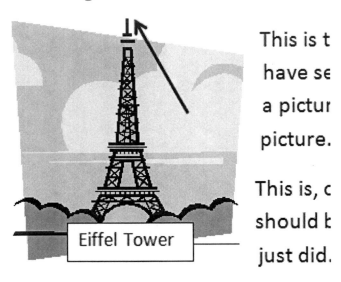

Figure 8-24. *Repositioned Arrow*

Add Informative Text Box

We've already added one text box. Now we're going to add another so that we can identify the height of the Eiffel Tower. In order to make the picture appear less crowded, we're going to use a smaller font. We've already shown you how to insert a text box and resize it, so we won't go over those details again. But, here are the steps:

1) Create a text box.
2) Type "986 ft." in the box.
3) Select the text in the box.
4) Click on the *Home* tab.

5) Select "**8**" as the font size in the *Font* group.
6) Resize the text box to fit the text in it.
7) Move the text box to the end of the arrow.

Your picture should now resemble ours.

Congratulations.

You've learned how to insert a picture and then enhance it to present information to the reader in a memorable way.

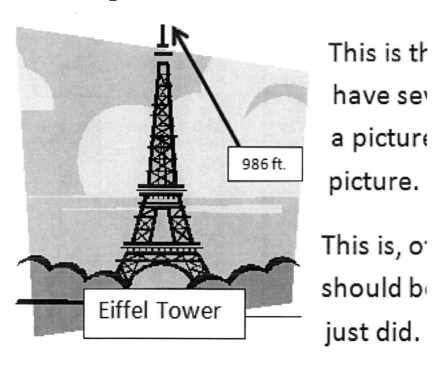

Figure 8-25. *Completed Tower Picture*

Summary

We hoped we've inspired you to learn more with text boxes and objects like arrows and to put them in your *Word 2010* documents. You can do a lot with text boxes and objects such as arrows, callouts, and other basic shapes, but explaining all of the options and commands would take a much longer book. If you're interested, we've supplied you with the basics. You can explore inserting *shape* objects, moving them around in your document, and changing the object properties. Use *Help* to learn about different commands in the different format ribbons.

In this chapter, we've shown you how to insert a text box. We've typed text into the text box, resized the box, and moved the box around on the page.

We've inserted an arrow, although we've shown you how to insert other objects. We've also shown you how to insert pictures. These can be pictures you've taken with your camera. One of the key points here is to know the folder location of your pictures. You could, of course, save them to your desktop.

With a simple arrow and a text box, you can turn a simple text document into a visually informative presentation. All you need to do is to become more familiar with these objects and integrate them into your work.

We've also shown you some picture enhancement commands, including the **Picture Layout**, **Background Removal**, and **Insert Screenshot** commands.

Chapter 9

■ ■ ■

Techniques with Tables

Introduction

Although the **Table** command is the only visible command in the *Tables* group, it is a powerful command. With it, you accomplish many features that require spacing on the page.

For example, if you're working solely with text, you can use the **tab** key to move your insertion point over to the right side of the page. But with a table, you can have areas of the table spread across your page, and you can put text or pictures in each.

Tables are also excellent tools to present information to the reader. Each column in a table, for example, could list the bills you pay each month. Or you could list inventory items in each room of your house. If you think about it, the month of a calendar is a table.

We'll show you how to insert tables, show you a few uses, and then it's up to your imagination and needs to come up with more ways to use your tables.

Insert a Table

Let's make this a project for home use. We'll point out how you could use it for a class paper as well, but we've found that, for some, knowledge acquired to produce a class paper can be quickly forgotten while knowledge acquired for the benefit of personal use can be more firmly ingrained.

And so let's assume for the moment that you want to make a list of chores for household members. Let's get started.

1) Open a new document.
2) Type the name of your document, "Household Chores".
3) Press **enter** 3 (or so) times.
4) Click on the *Insert* tab.
5) Find the *Tables* group.

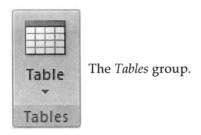

The *Tables* group.

The *Insert Table* dialog box appears.

Insert Table

Insert Table...

Draw Table

Convert Text to Table...

Excel Spreadsheet

Quick Tables   ▶

Figure 9-1. *The Insert Table Dialog Box*

You could select, using your pointer and left mouse button, boxes to indicate how many columns and rows you want. Just move your pointer over the top left box, press the left mouse button, and move your pointer to the right and down until your table is the size you desire. Then release the mouse button.

Instead, we're going to use the **Insert Table ...** command.

6) Select Insert Table ....

Another *Insert Table* dialog box appears. We've entered the number of columns we want (**4**) and the number of rows (**7**).

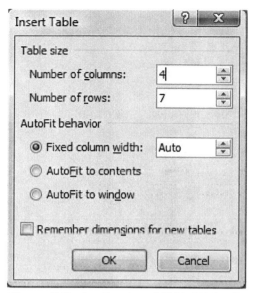

Figure 9-2. *Another Insert Table Dialog Box*

> 7) Enter 4 for Number of columns:.
> 8) Enter 7 for Number of rows:.
> 9) Press OK.

Click on the checkbox for *Remember dimensions for new tables* to have the same number of rows and columns for your next inserted table.

Your document should look similar to ours below. Notice that our table has lines for borders. Remember, when you insert a table, you might need to increase the number of rows by 1 if you want a header row (the same goes for columns). But don't worry. If you insert a table with too few rows (or columns), you can insert more later.

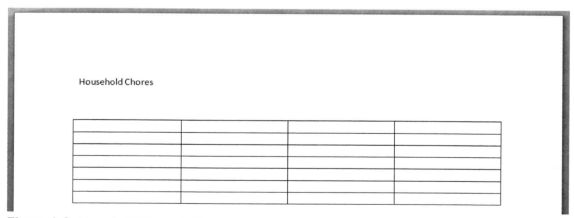

Figure 9-3. *Household Chores Table*

Also note that there are two new tabs. Because your table is selected, *Word* thinks you want to perform commands on it, so it gives you two tab options, *Design* and *Layout*.

Before we move on with working with our Household Chores table, we did want to point out one of the options that *Word 2010* offers.

It's in the **Insert Table** command offering. At the bottom of the drop-down menu is a command called Quick Tables. Click on Quick Tables and browse down the choices with the side bar. As you can see, you have the option of inserting preformatted tables.

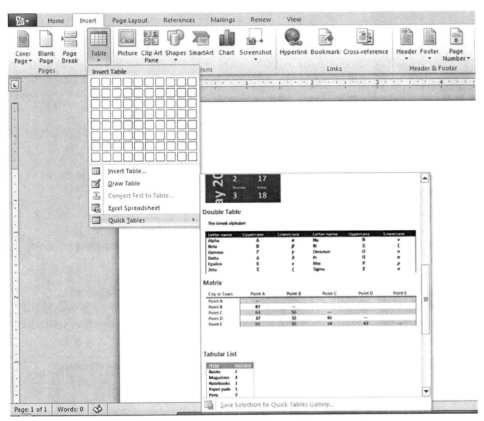

Figure 9-4. *Quick Table Menu*

But because we want to teach you some of the ways to manipulate tables, including how the rows and columns appear, we're going to continue with our Household Chores file.

Adding Text to Tables

Now we want to add our text to the Household Chores table. Note that each "box" in our table is called a cell. You can move around from cell to cell by moving your pointer to the cell you want and clicking the mouse button. You can also use the arrow keys on your keyboard.

Type "Jeremy", "Jill", and "Jason" in the top row cells, skipping the first column.

Type the days of the week, starting with "Monday" in the first column, skipping the first row. End with Saturday. (We're giving everyone Sunday off, so there'll be no Sunday chores.)

Select the first row by clicking and dragging your insertion point across it, or place your pointer in the left margin, beside the row, and left clicking. You'll know when the first row is selected because it will be highlighted.

Select the *Home* tab and click on **Center**. This centers the names in the cells.

Deselect the table by clicking elsewhere on the page.

Your table should now look like ours.

Household Chores

	Jeremy	Jill	Jason
Monday			
Tuesday			
Wednesday			
Thursday			
Friday			
Saturday			

Figure 9-5. *Table with Text*

You can work with the text in a table just like you can work with text that exists anywhere else in your document. You simply have to select the text.

Practice selecting a cell (and the text in it) by moving your pointer to the left side of a cell, near the border. The shape of your pointer might change, depending on your settings. When it is pointing at a cell, left click the mouse button. The cell becomes highlighted. Any text commands you choose will now affect the text within that selected cell.

Note that for a class paper, you could present other information in a table like this. For example, you could have a table titled *American Presidents by Century*.

You could have in the first row, *1700s, 1800s, 1900s,* and *2000s.* In each column, you could then place the name of a president in a cell.

Note that if your insertion point is in a cell, you can select the *Insert* tab, then select the **Picture** command to insert a picture into a cell in a table.

Let's take a step back for a moment and look at the two new ribbons that the **Insert Table** command has given you to work with.

We'll come back to our *Household Chores* document later in this chapter.

Table Design Ribbon

The *Design* tab gives you three groups on the ribbon: *Table Style Options*, *Table Styles*, and *Draw Borders*.

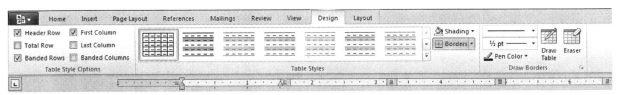

Figure 9-6. *Design Ribbon for Tables*

Click inside your table to put your insertion point in the table. The *Table* tabs become highlighted. Select the *Design* tab.

Now, move your pointer over the different *Table Styles* pictures of table in the center of the ribbon. As your pointer moves over each selection, the table in your document gives you a preview of what your table would look like if you select that style.

Notice that for our table, we have a "header" in the first row. This row highlights the names of the children. Our first column also has special significance in that it identifies days of the week. Why do we point this out?

Because if you'll notice the *Table Style Options* group, there are different checkboxes that you can select. These will affect how the *Table Style* appears. You might, for example, want groups of two rows grouped together with different background colors.

Practice checking different checkboxes and seeing how this affects your table as you move your pointer over the *Table Style* selections.

There are, though, a few commands we want to highlight on the *Table Design* ribbon. Here are a couple of commands in the *Table Styles* group.

- **Shading** When you select a cell, a row, a column, or any number of cells, you can select the shading of those selected cells with this command.

- **Borders** When you select cells, or the entire table, you can select the borders for the selection. Sometimes, for example, you might not want a border on the top or bottom of a cell.

The *Draw Borders* group has a few more commands of interest.

- **Pen Color** This command selects the color of the borders of the cells.
- **Draw Border** You can draw additional cells or tables by selecting this command. After selecting it, click and drag to draw additional cells. Don't worry, *Word* squares the cells for you.
- **Eraser** You can erase cells or rows or columns (or an entire table!) with this command. After selecting it, click and drag to erase.

One other command in the *Draw Borders* group allows you to select the style of the lines for the borders in your table. This is the box with a line in it. Use the selection arrow to choose another line style. The other command allows you to select the point (pt.) size of your lines.

Table Layout Ribbon

Let's take a look at the *Layout* ribbon for tables. We'll be using some of these commands for our *Household Chores* document, so we'll leave this *Layout* tab selected as we move forward.

Figure 9-7. *Layout Ribbon for Tables*

We'll go through these groups one at a time, starting with the *Table* group on the left.

- **Select** Opens a dialog box that allows you to select different parts of the table. After cells are selected, you can perform commands on the selected cells.
- **View Gridlines** If you remove all of the borders in your table, you can still see where the borders are via gridlines. They display onscreen but do not show on the printed document. This command allows you to view or hide the gridlines.
- **Properties** Select different properties of the table here via a pop-up dialog box, including text wrapping, text alignment, borders and other table properties. These commands are similar to the text box commands discussed earlier.

The *Rows & Columns* group allows you to insert rows and columns. Select a row or column, and then select the appropriate command. You can also delete row and columns with the **Delete** command. The *Merge* group allows you to merge multiple rows into one row and multiple columns into one column. It also allows you to split cells into multiple cells and to split rows into multiple rows.

Merging rows or columns can create formatting problems if there are different properties associated with each.

The *Cell Size* group allows you to choose the height and width of your selected cells. You can also choose to have the cells automatically conform to the size of the text in the cell with **Autofit**.

The *Alignment* group has picture commands to allow you to align the text to the left, middle, right, top, and bottom sides of the cell. There is also a **Cell Margins** command in this group. Select **Cell Margins** for a pop-up dialog box that allows you to choose the distance that your text appears from the border of the cell.

The *Data* group is for advanced users who want to fill their tables with numbers and to sort them and to perform math functions on them.

Household Chores

Let's go back to house *Household Chores* document. Select the first row and select **Bold** from the *Font* group under the *Home* tab. Type in chores such as 1) *Take garbage out*, 2) *Sweep floors*, and 3) *Wash dishes*. Select the cells with chores in them and select **Center** in the *Paragraph* group.
Your document should resemble ours.

Household Chores

	Jeremy	**Jill**	**Jason**
Monday	Wash dishes	Take garbage out	Sweep floors
Tuesday	Sweep floors	Wash dishes	Take garbage out
Wednesday	Take garbage out	Sweep floors	Wash dishes
Thursday	Wash dishes	Take garbage out	Sweep floors
Friday	Sweep floors	Wash dishes	Take garbage out
Saturday	Take garbage out	Sweep floors	Wash dishes

Figure 9-8. *Table with Chores*

If you wanted to make your table color coded, for example, you could assign a color to each chore. You could select each cell with *Wash dishes* in it and give that cell a red background. You could select blue for *Sweep floors* and green for *Take garbage out*.

For the final touches on our table, we're going to increase the cell size so that our table doesn't look so cramped. We'll also select a different right border on the first column to set apart the days of the week from the cells with chores.

1) Select the table by putting insertion point in it.
2) Click **Select**.
3) Click on **Select Table**.
4) Select the *Layout* tab.
5) Click on up arrow in **Cell Height** until **0.4"** is shown.
6) Click on **Align Center** in the *Alignment* group. (Center horizontally and vertically.)
7) Select the first column in the table.
8) Click on the *Design* tab.
9) Select **1½ pt**.
10) Select **Borders**. A dialog box appears.
11) Select **Right Border**.
12) Deselect the table.

Your table should look like ours.

Household Chores

	Jeremy	Jill	Jason
Monday	Wash dishes	Take garbage out	Sweep floors
Tuesday	Sweep floors	Wash dishes	Take garbage out
Wednesday	Take garbage out	Sweep floors	Wash dishes
Thursday	Wash dishes	Take garbage out	Sweep floors
Friday	Sweep floors	Wash dishes	Take garbage out
Saturday	Take garbage out	Sweep floors	Wash dishes

Figure 9-9. *Formatted Table with Chores*

Congratulations!

You're on your way to becoming proficient with using tables. While you have your document open, select other commands to become more familiar with tables. Remember to save your document. You wouldn't be the first person to lose work because a document hasn't been saved and there is a power failure or computer crash.

Summary

In this chapter, we learned how to insert tables into a document. We learned how to insert text into cells within a table.

We took our table and learned how to use the *Design* ribbon to change the appearance of our table. Additionally, we used the *Layout* ribbon to select other commands for our table, such as aligning text within the cells.

Cell borders can be different colors and constructed with thicker point sizes. Cells can be shaded with different colors to provide visual enhancement. Color codes can also be used by creative *Word* users to present more order to the information in their tables.

You can increase the point size of the lines that form the borders of table cells. You can also adjust the distance from the borders to the text.

The height of rows can be increased or decreased. There are also commands to adjust the width of columns. These are useful when the text appears too crowded in a table.

Remember, you can also insert pictures into your cells. If you create a table with two columns, you could insert pictures into the cells in the left column. In the right column, you could write descriptions of the pictures.

Chapter 10

■ ■ ■

Techniques to Create a Resume

Introduction

Many of the commands we'll talk about in this chapter have already been discussed in this book. This chapter will bring many of those elements together. With some books on how to work with *Word*, you get nothing but descriptions of commands. Other books are more like exercise books, presenting problems and letting the reader figure out how to do it.

We're going to show you how to write a resume from scratch with *Microsoft Word 2010*. We'll show you briefly how to opt for a resume template, but that's not how we're going to make ours. While constructing our resume, you'll see how the commands we use affect the text and how to use table commands to manipulate tables.

Right away, we're going to start with a table, which we described in the last chapter. Our resume will have two columns. The left column will list the categories such as work experience and education. The column on the right will host the details.

Along the way, we'll work with *tabs* and **Font** commands.

We encourage you to work along with us while we construct a resume. If you're a student, this will be great practice for when you graduate and begin your job hunt. If you're currently looking for employment, you can improve your existing resume or come up with one that outshines the one you currently have. If you're employed …, well, it never hurts to have an updated resume on file … just in case. And if you opt for a building your resume from a resume template, then following along will help you to work with that template.

New File

We're going to walk through this, step by step. So far in this book, we've encouraged you to repeat the process we used at the start, using the Blank document command. This time, we're going to show you a twist.

1) Click on the **Office** button., which takes you to the Backstage view.
2) Select **New**.

The *Available Templates* command pane appears.

Figure 10-1. *Templates Available Command Pane*

We have throughout this book instructed you to select **Blank document**. This time is different. We will go back and open a blank document in order to create our resume, but it is useful to see how the template process works.

3) **Click on Resumes.**

Browse through the templates, keeping in mind you might want to use one later. Templates can be great time savers. These documents open with formats and tables already established.

Note that the choices you encounter may vary if you're connected to the Internet or not. Also, the appearance can vary if you've already opened a template. After you select **Resumes**, another screen appears.

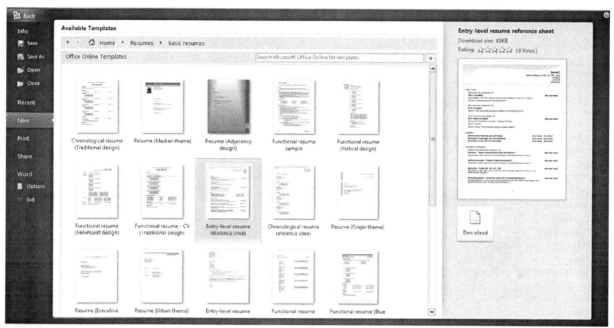

Figure 10-2. *Resume Templates*

We have clicked once on entry-level resume reference sheet. Note that a screenshot of the template appears in the right-most pane.

If you were to double-click on the entry-level resume reference sheet, the template would open as a *Word* file. You would enter your data and save the file as a *Word* document. Make sure you don't save it as a template. We suggest saving it immediately as a *Word* document in a folder location you're familiar with.

When you open the template, a *Help* pane opens, too. This pane can help answer your questions with working on the file.

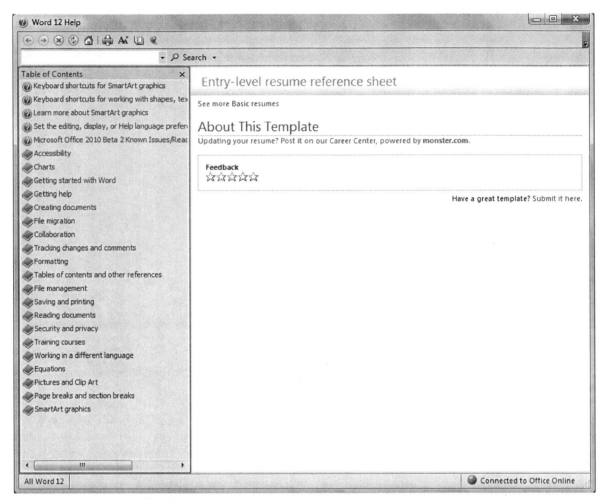

Figure 10-3. *Template Word Help*

 You may run across a template with the letters CV in the name. In case you didn't know, a CV stands for *Curriculum Vitae*, which is basically a more detailed resume that lists published works and other items in a career.

Instead of the reference sheet, we've opened a basic chronological resume. Type in your data in the fields provided to complete your resume the easy way.

[Street Address], [City, ST ZIP Code]•[phone]•[e-mail]

[Your Name]

Objective

[Describe your career goal or ideal job.]

Experience

[Dates of employment]   [Company Name]   [City, ST]

[Job Title]
- [Job responsibility/achievement]
- [Job responsibility/achievement]
- [Job responsibility/achievement]

[Dates of employment]   [Company Name]   [City, ST]

[Job Title]
- [Job responsibility/achievement]
- [Job responsibility/achievement]
- [Job responsibility/achievement]

[Dates of employment]   [Company Name]   [City, ST]

[Job Title]

Figure 10-4. *Chronological Resume Template*

We shorted the template to fit it in the picture, but you get the idea. Simply place your insertion point in the template and delete existing text and replace it with your own.

Remember to save it as a document and not as a template!

Create a Resume

By creating our own resume, we'll be able to go over many of the commands we've already covered in this book and cover a few more that we believe you'll find useful.

1) Click on the *Office* button to go to the Backstage view.
2) Select **New**.
3) Click on **Blank document**.
4) Select **Create** (or double-click on **Blank document**).
5) Select the *Insert* tab.
6) Select **Table**.
7) Select **Insert Table ....**
8) Select **2** columns and **6** rows.
9) Click on **OK**.

You should have a document that resembles ours.

Figure 10-5. _New Document with Table_

Name and Address

In a way, we're starting out with our own template. We have the cells on the page in which we're going to enter our resume. Keep in mind that there are hundreds, if not thousands, of ways to put your resume together. We're just going to put one together. Use your imagination to come up with your own design if you're so inclined.

1) Type your name in the first row, first column cell.
2) Click and drag to select the text in your name or simply select the cell.
3) Select the _Home_ tab and change the font size to **20**.
4) Select **Bold** to put your name in bold text.
5) Select the first row, second column cell.
6) With the cell selected, place a left tab at the 4.5" mark on the ruler.
7) Place insertion point in the first row, first column cell.
8) Press **ctrl** and **tab** at the same time.

When your insertion point is in a table, pressing tab moves your insertion point to the next cell. By pressing **ctrl** and **tab** at the same time, your insertion point moves to the tab we just established.

9) Type your street address.
10) Press enter.
11) Press ctrl and tab at the same time.
12) Type your city, state, and zip code.
13) Press tab to move your insertion point to the next cell.

While your insertion point is still in the first row, second column, you can add additional contact information such as your telephone number and email address. Simply press **enter** for a new line and then press **ctrl** and **tab** at the same.

Your document should resemble ours. Don't worry; we'll get rid of the lines later. We wouldn't want them our resume, so we don't expect you'll want them in yours.

Jill or John Q. Public	123 Main Street AnyCity, AnyState 12345

Figure 10-6. *Contact Information in Resume*

Add Spacing

We don't want the *Objective* part of our resume, which will go in the second row, to crowd our contact information in the first row. We could insert some blank rows, or we could press enter several times to get our desired space. Instead, we're going to select a command that will place our second-row text one inch from the top border.

> 1) Select the second row in the table.
> 2) Select the *Home* tab.
> 3) Click on the **Launcher** (the arrow in the bottom right corner) of the *Paragraph* group.
> 4) Under the Spacing command selections, select **30 pt** for **Before:**.
> 5) Click on **OK**.
> 6) Place your insertion point in the second row, first column.
> 7) Type "Objective".
> 8) Press **tab** to move to the second column.
> 9) Type your career or job objective.

Your document should look like ours.

Jill or John Q. Public	123 Main Street AnyCity, AnyState 12345
Objective	To get a job working with widgets and gadgets.

Figure 10-7. *Objective in Resume*

Row Formatting

We have good spacing now between the body of our resume and our contact information. But we have a problem. The word "Objective" is far to the left of the page. It's difficult to connect the word with our actual typed-in objective. Also, it seems like having two columns of equal width isn't the correct way to proceed. After all, one column is going to have very few words, objective, education, etc, while the second column is going to have a lot of information.

It would be nice if we could make the first column more narrow, starting with the second row. And then align the first column text farther to the left.

Aha! We can do accomplish these tasks easily.

1) Select all of the rows except the first by pressing the left mouse button and dragging the pointer down, starting with the second row.
2) Move the pointer over the center table border indicator on the horizontal ruler. A helper text box appears with the words "Move Table Column" appears.

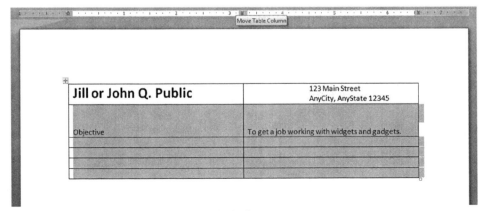

Figure 10-8. *Column Border Adjust in Ruler*

Press the mouse button and move the border to the left, aligning it with the period after "Q" in John Q. Public.

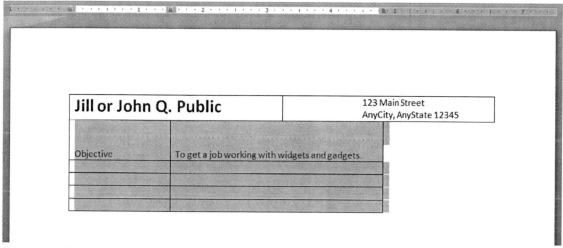

Figure 10-9. *Narrowed First Column*

This is how we wanted the first column to look, but now the right border of our second column has also moved to the left.

Note that we have not deselected the rows yet. Rows 2 through row 6 are still selected. If you deselected them, click and drag to select the rows again because we're going to move the right border of those rows.

> 3) Move the cursor to the horizontal ruler and place it over the right border indicator. "Move Table Column" appears.

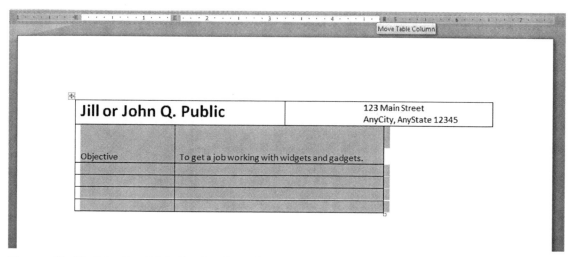

Figure 10-10. *Selecting Right Border Control*

4) Press the left mouse button and move the border to the right until it is aligned with the right border of the first row.
5) Deselect the rows by clicking elsewhere on the page.

Your document should resemble ours.

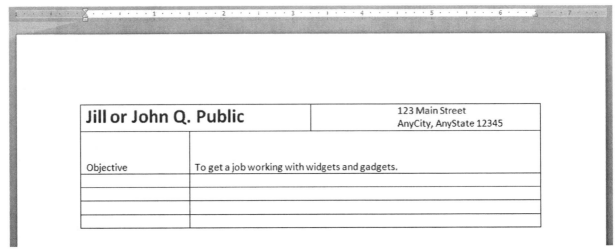

Figure 10-11. *Re-sized Columns*

Our resume is starting to look good. If we can move the word "Objective" over to the right a little, we'll be happy with our alignment.

Looking ahead, we'll want the other words in our first column, such as "education" and "work experience", to have the same alignment, so we're going to select the first column, minus the cell in the first row. We'll have to make this selection by using our pointer, clicking in the second row, first column, dragging down the bottom of the first row, then releasing the mouse button. Then we'll add a tab to align the text to the right.

6) Select the cells in the first column, minus the first row cell.
7) Click on the tab select button at the left end of the horizontal ruler until the right tab appears.
8) Click on the ruler at the 1" mark. Note this places a tab in the first column.

Your document should look like ours. Note the tab marker in the ruler.

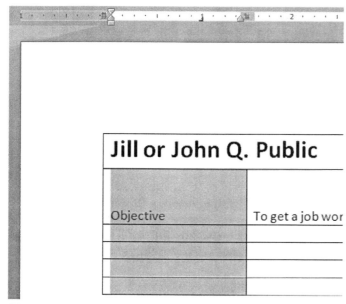

Figure 10-12. *Right Tab in First Column*

Okay, now we're ready to take advantage of the tab we just inserted.

> 9) Deselect the cells.
> 10) Place the insertion point at the start of the word "Objective" in the first column, second row.
> 11) Press **ctrl** and **tab** at the same time. (Remember, pressing tab in a table moves the insertion point to the next cell, and we want to align text to a tab setting. **Ctrl** and **tab** does this.)

Finally! Now your resume is in very good shape and should look like ours. The rest of the text will be easily typed in.

Jill or John Q. Public	123 Main Street AnyCity, AnyState 12345
Objective	To get a job working with widgets and gadgets.

Figure 10-13. *Aligned Column Text*

Now, we need to add some spacing between the rest of our rows, but we don't want the large gap that was needed beneath our contact information. And so we'll go back to the *Paragraph* group after selecting our remaining rows.

Add More Spacing

As we prepare to write the rest of our resume, we want a little space between our *Objective* and our *Work Experience* sections.

How do we accomplish this?

The same way we added space before the *Objective* row. Only this time, we're going to select the four remaining rows and add space before each row. This will make our resume appear consistent and give it a smooth, professional feel. It will present another problem with spacing, but we'll show you how to correct the problem, and at the same time give you more experience with working with *Word*.

1) Select the bottom four rows by clicking and dragging.
2) Click on the *Home* tab.
3) Click on the *Paragraph* group's **Launcher**.
4) Select **18 pt** in the **Space before:** command window. You can click on the up and down arrows until **18** appears in the window or simply type **18** into the window.

Your document should look like ours.

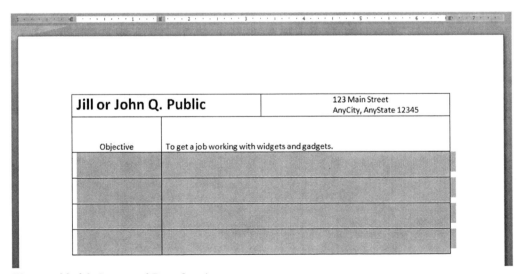

Figure 10-14. *Increased Row Spacing*

Note that our four rows are still selected. You can also notice that the border indicators are present in the ruler. Note the first column's right border indicator is showing up for the selected rows and *not* the first row.

Add Topic Text

Let's add the resume topics in the first column. Remember, we've already set a tab for these cells, and all of our topics will be right-aligned with *Objective*.

1) Click in the first cell below *Objective* to place your insertion point there.
2) Press **ctrl** and **tab** at the same time.
3) Type "Education".
4) Move your insertion point down one cell by clicking, pressing tab twice, or using the down arrow key.
5) Press **ctrl** and **tab** at the same time.
6) Type "Work Experience".
7) Move your insertion point down one cell by clicking, pressing tab twice, or using the down arrow key.
8) Press **ctrl** and **tab** at the same time.
9) Type "Computer Skills".
10) Move your insertion point down one cell by clicking, pressing tab twice, or using the down arrow key.
11) Press **ctrl** and **tab** at the same time.
12) Type "Hobbies".

Your document should look like ours.

Jill or John Q. Public		123 Main Street AnyCity, AnyState 12345
Objective	To get a job working with widgets and gadgets.	
Education		
Work Experience		
Computer Skills		
Hobbies		

Figure 10-15. *Resume Topics Entered*

Entering Education Text

Now that our (neatly aligned) resume topics are all set, we need to enter the text for our topics. We're not going to go through line by line and instruct you what to type. But keep in mind that you can set tabs in each cell. You can press enter in each cell. You can add bulleted lists to each cell.

For the Education topic, we've added tabs and entered our college, city in which the college was located, the diploma/certificate earned, and the year it was earned. When we press enter, however, we see that we have a large gap between our college listings.

Jill or John Q. Public		123 Main Street AnyCity, AnyState 12345	
Objective	To get a job working with widgets and gadgets.		
Education	Gadget College	Gadget City, AnyState	two-year diploma, 2008
	Widget College	Widget City, AnyState	trade certificate, 2009
Work Experience			
Computer Skills			
Hobbies			

Figure 10-16. *Education Text*

We need to correct the spacing in this cell.

1) Select the second line of text in the cell.
2) Click on the *Home* tab.
3) Click on the *Paragraph* group's **Launcher**.
4) Select **6 pt** in the **Space before:** command window. You can click on the up and down arrows until **6** appears in the window or simply type **6** into the window.

Congratulations. Your second line of text in the Education cell moves up.

We use this trick of paragraph spacing often with our work, especially with one-page documents that we're creating for a single use.

Check to see if your document looks like ours.

Jill or John Q. Public	123 Main Street AnyCity, AnyState 12345	
Objective	To get a job working with widgets and gadgets.	
Education	Gadget College Gadget City, AnyState two-year diploma, 2008 Widget College Widget City, AnyState trade certificate, 2009	
Work Experience		
Computer Skills		
Hobbies		

Figure 10-17. *Properly Spaced Education Text*

Let's move on to *Work Experience* and *Computer Skills*. Let's put bulleted lists in these. After we enter the text and get the spacing right, we'll move to our last row, Hobbies, and then get rid of those lines. We hope that during this process you're beginning to see how to view a document page and imagine where text can (or should) go on the page, and then by using your imagination, you can come up with *Word* commands to allow you to achieve your goals.

Text for Work Experience and Computer Skills

We're only going to enter three items each for work experience and computer skills. Your resume might have less or more items. But we are going to ask that for one of your items, use enough text that it will use text wrapping within the cell; that is, the sentence will run up against the right border of the cell and will automatically wrap around to the next line at the left border of the cell. For us, we'll do this with the first item in our Work Experience cell. We'll combine the steps below for each cell.

Position your insertion point in the *Work Experience* or *Computer Skills* cell.

1) Type in text for your first item. For the *Work Experience* cell, try to think of enough text that it text wraps (that is, it is longer that the width of the cell).
2) Press **enter**.
3) Type in text for your second item.
4) Press **enter**.
5) Type in text for your third item.

Your document should resemble ours. We want you to note that the spacing in the first item in the *Work Experience* cell looks good. That's because we have placed extra spacing (via the *Paragraph* group's **Launcher**) before each paragraph (a new paragraph starts when enter is pressed) and not before each line of text.

Jill or John Q. Public		123 Main Street AnyCity, AnyState 12345	
Objective	To get a job working with widgets and gadgets.		
Education	Gadget College	Gadget City, AnyState	two-year diploma, 2008
	Widget College	Widget City, AnyState	trade certificate, 2009
Work Experience	Worked as an associated widget maker and Widget Maker Enterprises, including big widgets and small widgets. 2007 - present		
	Assembled gadgets on the assembly line at Gadget Industries. 2006-2007		
	Designed widgets and gadgets for W&G Online for an internship. summer 2008		
Computer Skills	Extensive knowledge of Widget Computer Design application		
	Partial experience with Gadget On The Web designs		
	Working knowledge of document writing applications		
Hobbies			

Figure 10-18. *Work Experience and Computer Skills Text*

Let's correct the spacing between the second and third items in the Work Experience cell.

6) Select the second and third lines in the Work Experience cell.
7) Click on the Home tab.
8) Click on the Paragraph group's Launcher.
9) Select 6 pt in the Space before: command window. You can click on the up and down arrows until 6 appears in the window or simply type 6 into the window.
10) Deselect the text.

Look at our document and see how the spacing has changed in the Work Experience cell. You can change the spacing to whatever looks best to you.

Jill or John Q. Public		123 Main Street AnyCity, AnyState 12345	
Objective	To get a job working with widgets and gadgets.		
Education	Gadget College	Gadget City, AnyState	two-year diploma, 2008
	Widget College	Widget City, AnyState	trade certificate, 2009
Work Experience	Worked as an associated widget maker and Widget Maker Enterprises, including big widgets and small widgets. 2007 - present		
	Assembled gadgets on the assembly line at Gadget Industries. 2006-2007		
	Designed widgets and gadgets for W&G Online for an internship. summer 2008		
Computer Skills	Extensive knowledge of Widget Computer Design application		
	Partial experience with Gadget On The Web designs		
	Working knowledge of document writing applications		
Hobbies			

Figure 10-19. *Work Experience Text with Corrected Spacing*

Let's make our *Computers Skills* text a bulleted list. We'll do this in the next section.

Computer Skills Text

You will notice as we make the text in our Computer Skills cell a bulleted list, the text will become spaced correctly. That's because bulleted lists have their own spacing rules.

That's fine. It saves us from having to change spacing between lines.

1) Select the text in the Computer Skills cell.
2) Click on the *Home* tab.
3) Select **Bullets**. (Choose style of bulleted list if necessary.)

Your document should now look like ours. Note the spacing of the bullets.

Jill or John Q. Public		123 Main Street AnyCity, AnyState 12345	
Objective	To get a job working with widgets and gadgets.		
Education	Gadget College	Gadget City, AnyState	two-year diploma, 2008
	Widget College	Widget City, AnyState	trade certificate, 2009
Work Experience	Worked as an associated widget maker and Widget Maker Enterprises, including big widgets and small widgets. 2007 - present		
	Assembled gadgets on the assembly line at Gadget Industries. 2006-2007		
	Designed widgets and gadgets for W&G Online for an internship. summer 2008		
Computer Skills	• Extensive knowledge of Widget Computer Design application • Partial experience with Gadget On The Web designs • Working knowledge of document writing applications		
Hobbies			

Figure 10-20. *Bulleted Computer Skills Cell*

Hobbies Text

There are many different types of resumes. Some people like resumes that add a personal touch, especially if the personal items support a professional demeanor or add to the possible skill sets that an employer might be looking for.

1) Place your insertion point in the *Hobbies* cell.
2) Type three hobbies or personal interests, pressing enter after each hobby or interest.
3) Select the three lines of text in the *Hobbies* cell.
4) Click on the *Home* tab.
5) Select **Bullets**. (Choose style of bulleted list if necessary.)
6) Deselect the text.

Your resume should look like ours. Note how the spacing appears good, but we still have those lines, which we definitely do not want in our final copy.

Jill or John Q. Public		123 Main Street AnyCity, AnyState 12345
Objective	To get a job working with widgets and gadgets.	
Education	Gadget College Gadget City, AnyState two-year diploma, 2008 Widget College Widget City, AnyState trade certificate, 2009	
Work Experience	Worked as an associated widget maker and Widget Maker Enterprises, including big widgets and small widgets. 2007 - present Assembled gadgets on the assembly line at Gadget Industries. 2006-2007 Designed widgets and gadgets for W&G Online for an internship. summer 2008	
Computer Skills	• Extensive knowledge of Widget Computer Design application • Partial experience with Gadget On The Web designs • Working knowledge of document writing applications	
Hobbies	• Enjoy reading Gadget Weekly magazine. • Make widgets every month in garage hobby bench. • Wrote *All Work and No Play Makes Jack a Dull Boy* under the pseudonym of Jack Torrance, a novel published by the Overlook Hotel publishing company.	

Figure 10-21. *Bulleted Hobbies Cell*

Removing Lines

Let's remove the lines from our resume. First we're going to remove the lines that would print if we printed our resume. Then we'll remove the gridlines, which don't print, so you can see what your final document will look like when you send it via email or print.

1) Place insertion point in the table (anywhere).
2) Click on the *Layout* tab in *Table Tools*.
3) Click on **Properties**.
4) Click on the **Borders and Shading ...** button.
5) Click on **None** in **Setting**.
6) Click on **OK**.
7) Deselect the table by clicking elsewhere.

Your resume should look like ours.

Note that the lines have been replaced by dotted lines, which are called gridlines so you can see the location of the table cells.

Jill or John Q. Public		123 Main Street AnyCity, AnyState 12345
Objective	To get a job working with widgets and gadgets.	
Education	Gadget College Gadget City, AnyState Widget College Widget City, AnyState	two-year diploma, 2008 trade certificate, 2009
Work Experience	Worked as an associated widget maker and Widget Maker Enterprises, including big widgets and small widgets. 2007 - present Assembled gadgets on the assembly line at Gadget Industries. 2006-2007 Designed widgets and gadgets for W&G Online for an internship. summer 2008	
Computer Skills	• Extensive knowledge of Widget Computer Design application • Partial experience with Gadget On The Web designs • Working knowledge of document writing applications	
Hobbies	• Enjoy reading Gadget Weekly magazine. • Make widgets every month in garage hobby bench. • Wrote *All Work and No Play Makes Jack a Dull Boy* under the pseudonym of Jack Torrance, a novel published by the Overlook Hotel publishing company.	

Figure 10-22. *Lines Removed from Resume*

Remove Dotted Lines (Gridlines)
Now all we have to do is remove the gridlines.

1) Place your insertion point in the table (anywhere).
2) Click on the *Layout* tab in *Table Tools*.
3) Click on **Select** in the Table group.
4) Click on **Select Table**.
5) Click on **Properties** in the Table group.
6) Click on **Borders and Shading ...**.
7) Select **None** in **Setting:**.
8) Click on **View Gridlines** (if your gridlines are present).

Your resume should now look like ours.

Congratulations. You've come a long way in working with *Word 2010*. Your resume is proof.

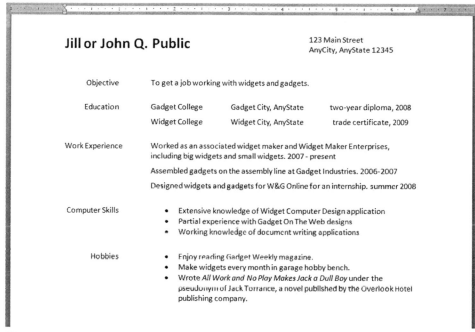

Jill or John Q. Public   123 Main Street
                                              AnyCity, AnyState 12345

Objective   To get a job working with widgets and gadgets.

Education   Gadget College   Gadget City, AnyState   two-year diploma, 2008

                 Widget College   Widget City, AnyState   trade certificate, 2009

Work Experience Worked as an associated widget maker and Widget Maker Enterprises,
                 including big widgets and small widgets. 2007 - present

                 Assembled gadgets on the assembly line at Gadget Industries. 2006-2007

                 Designed widgets and gadgets for W&G Online for an internship. summer 2008

Computer Skills   • Extensive knowledge of Widget Computer Design application
                    • Partial experience with Gadget On The Web designs
                    • Working knowledge of document writing applications

Hobbies   • Enjoy reading Gadget Weekly magazine.
                    • Make widgets every month in garage hobby bench.
                    • Wrote *All Work and No Play Makes Jack a Dull Boy* under the
                      pseudonym of Jack Torrance, a novel published by the Overlook Hotel
                      publishing company.

Figure 10-23. *Resume with No Lines*

Chapter Summary

In this chapter, we brought together many of the previous lessons in order to construct a resume.

We started with opening a new document. We have been starting with blank documents, but we showed you how to open a document based on a preexisting template. Templates are great ways to have tables and formatting already set for your needs. But we went with a blank document in order to show you how to manipulate text and tables.

We used text formatting commands, such as **Bold**. We showed you how to resize your text.

Tabs were used to position text in the table cells. We used a right-justify tab in order to place text at the right end of a cell.

In summary, this chapter brought together the lessons learned in this book. We hope that you can use the knowledge in order to benefit you directly, whether by a resume that gets you a job or a letter that gets you admitted into the college of your choice.

Chapter 11

■ ■ ■

Odds and Ends Techniques

Introduction

We wanted to take the opportunity in this last chapter to cover some topics that have not yet appeared in this book. There are several reasons for this, but it's not because we don't use the topics in this chapter. In fact, some of these topics cover commands that we most often use in *Word 2010*. We will cover our favorite topics, our most-used commands, and other bits of trivia with Word. Then we'll talk about what we hope you take away from a book like this, and what we hope we've been able to teach you during the passing of these pages.

So, let's get started on this last chapter.

Zoom

With computer monitors coming in so many sizes and people having eyesight that may or may not be impeccable, it is nice to have a command to magnify the document on which you're working. Using Zoom won't change the way the document appears when it is printed. The only change is how the document appears on the monitor. Think of it as taking out your magnifying glass and looking at your document.

Everything becomes …, well, magnified.

Let's see how it works.

> 1) Open a new document.
> 2) Type some text.

Here's what our text looks like.

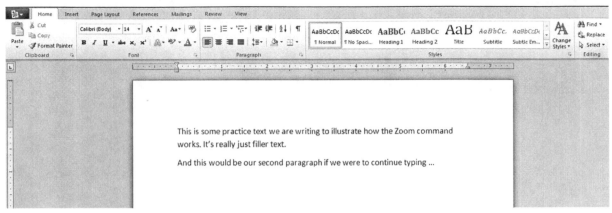

Figure 11-1. *Default Magnification*

     3) Select the *View* tab.
     4) Click on **Zoom**.

Note there are different settings you can choose. Try out different ones to see what effect they have. We like using **Page Width** because it gives us a little magnification while being able to see much of the page onscreen.

     5) Click on the **Page Width** radio button.
     6) Click **OK**.

Your document should look like ours.

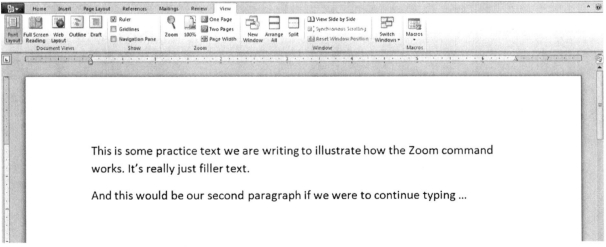

Figure 11-2. *Page Width Magnification*

Let's see what 200% magnification looks like.

7) Select **Zoom**.
8) Click on **200%** radio button.
9) Click **OK**.

This is what our document looks like.

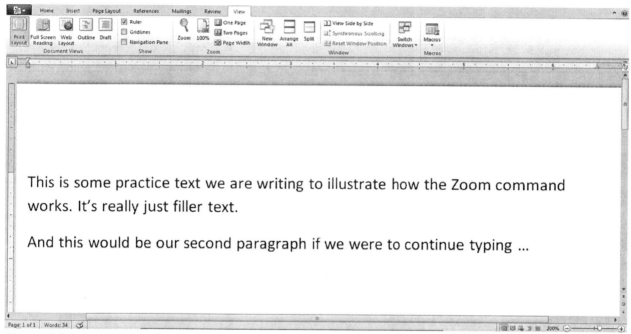

Figure 11-3. *200% Magnification*

Let's cover one more setting.

The Whole Page radio button is a useful setting when you want to see the entire page so you can position pictures or other objects on the page and see the results at a glance. It might be difficult to read text in this setting, but for the DO NOT ENTER sign, it is a useful setting.

Go back to the Zoom command and select Whole Page.

Here's what our document looks like.

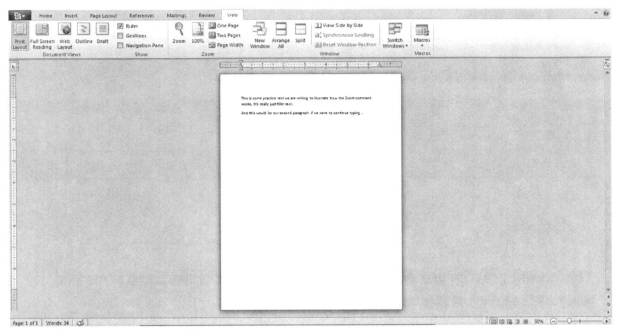

Figure 11-4. *Whole Page Magnification*

We hope you find a Zoom setting that suits both your needs and your eyesight.

Keyboard Shortcuts.

We would like to go over a few keyboard shortcuts.

A keyboard shortcut is a command that takes effect because of the keys that you press. It's called a shortcut because you could select the command by going to the ribbon, finding the command, and clicking on it.

But sometimes pressing keys is quicker, especially if you use the command a lot.

We'll give you four of the keyboard shortcuts that we use daily. And we rarely use any others. That's not to say others aren't useful; they're just not useful to us.

ctrl + c	**Copy** Highlight text (or a picture or any object) and press **ctrl** and **c** at the same time. Word copies the selection to the clipboard.
ctrl + x	**Cut** This command deletes the selection (text or picture) and places it on the clipboard.
ctrl + v	**Paste** Whether you have cut or copied text (or a picture), this command pastes it into the document at the insertion point.

ctrl + z   **Undo** This command undoes your last command.

Insert Symbol

Sometimes there are symbols we want to put into our document that are not on the keyboard. For example, we might want to insert a copyright symbol, or ©.

Or we might need a small circle to indicate temperate, the degree symbol, as in 75 °F.

In order to insert these symbols, and any other available symbols, we simply have to know where to look. Symbols like the copyright symbol are more commonly used, so to find the degree symbol we have to look a little farther.

Use the same Word document that we used for the **Zoom** command (or open a new document).

   1) Click on the *Insert* tab.
   2) Click on **Symbol** in the *Symbols* group.

You'll see a choice of commonly used symbols you can select from the pop-up dialog box.

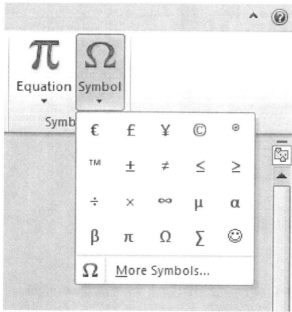

Figure 11-5. *Commonly Used Symbols*

   3) Click on the copyright symbol.

The copyright symbol inserts automatically. Now move your insertion point to where you want to insert the degree symbol. Then follow these steps.

> 4) Click on the *Insert* tab.
> 5) Click on **Symbol** in the *Symbols* group.
> 6) Click on **More Symbols ....**

A new dialog box will open with a scroll bar. You can scroll down the choices to find the symbol you want. For us, the degree symbol is near the top of the choices so we don't have to do any scrolling.

Note our highlighted box in the following picture. "DEGREE SIGN" appears in text near the bottom left of the dialog box to tell us what we've selected.

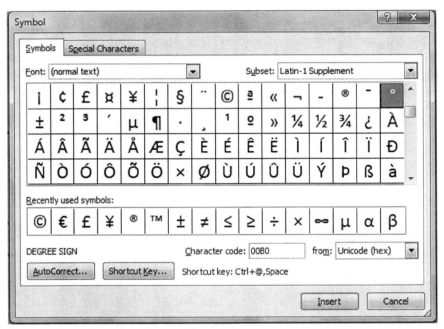

Figure 11-6. *More Symbols and Degree Sign*

> 7) Find the *degree* symbol and select it by clicking on it.
> 8) Click on **Insert**.
> 9) Click on **Close**.

You can see how we've inserted these symbols into our document below. Look through the symbol choices to see what's available.

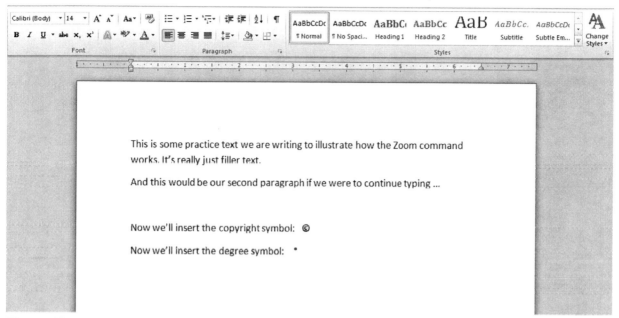

Figure 11-7. *Inserted Copyright and Degree Symbols*

As a final note for this section, you might have noticed when you clicked on **More Symbols**, there was an additional tab selection available. This tab was titled *Special Characters*.

We just wanted to point this out to you in case you wish to insert *M dashes* or other symbols such as a *non-breaking hyphen* (the hyphen and all of the hyphenated word(s) will text wrap to the next line instead of text wrapping at the hyphen).

1) Go ahead and select **Symbol** from the *Insert* ribbon.
2) Select **More Symbols**.
3) Click on the *Special Characters* tab.

Here are some of the special characters available for insertion. Note there's a slide-bar to scroll down for more options.

Figure 11-8. *Special Characters*

So, now that you're well acquainted with inserting symbols and special characters, let's move on to *WordArt*.

WordArt

WordArt is a fancy name for an application that *Word* used to present your text in a graphical image. Many of the commands that are available in *WordArt* can be accessed through the **Text Effects** command.

WordArt, though, gives you an object that can be moved around in the document.
This could be an excellent method to create a flyer. By the way, there are templates that you can use for fliers, also.

For now, we're just going to show you how to make a *Family Reunion* announcement with *WordArt*.

> 1) Open a new document.
> 2) Click on the *Insert* tab.

 Whenever you create a new document, consider hitting **enter** a few times before starting your typing. This gives you lines above your work in case you want to add text later. You can always delete these lines later.

> 3) Click on **WordArt** in the *Text* group.

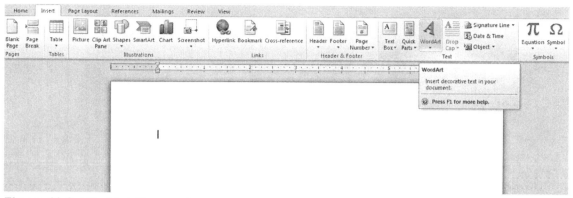

Figure 11-9. *WordArt Command*

After you select **WordArt**, a dialog box opens. This box presents you with choices for the style of text you want to use.

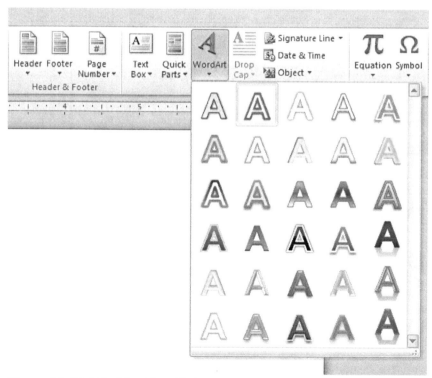

Figure 11-10. *WordArt Text Choices*

    4) Select a text style of *WordArt* by clicking on one of the choices.

An *Edit WordArt Text* box appears. This is the box in which you type your text.

Figure 11-11. *Enter WordArt Text*

    5) Type your text.
    6) Click **OK**.

Here is our document after typing in our text. Note the new *Format* ribbon.

Figure 11-12. *WordArt Text*

There are many different commands for formatting your text and changing its appearance.

We invite you to explore some of the different commands.

We'll show you one of these commands. First, select all of your text by placing your insertion point in the text object. Then select all of the text with the keyboard shortcut, **Ctrl + A**. Select **Text Effects**, which will present you with a drop-down menu, and then select **Transform**.

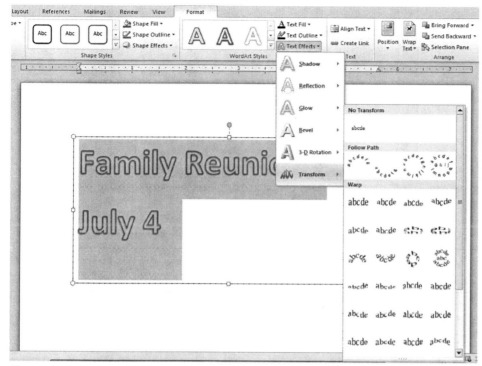

Figure 11-13. *Transform Command*

Here is what our final text looks like after:

- a) Centering our text
- b) Transforming the text to a semicircular desing
- c) Adding a fill color to the text
- d) Adding a glow to the shape.

Figure 11-14. *Family Reunion in WordArt*

Remember that your *WordArt* text is like a picture. You can select it, which will show you the handles. Click and drag on a handle and you can make your *WordArt* bigger or smaller. You can also rotate it by selecting the object and then moving the green handle on top to the left or to the right.

You can also perform any of the other commands on a *WordArt* object as you can other objects or pictures.

Conclusion

We showed you some odds and ends techniques in this last chapter of our book. We pointed out some keyboard shortcuts, a few ways to liven up your documents by using *WordArt*, how to view your documents more closely via the **Zoom** command, and how to insert symbols and special characters.

We hope that this book has helped you to learn word processing techniques of *Microsoft Word 2010*. It is a powerful program. Sometimes there seem to be too many commands, and the ribbons can be intimidating.

But by remembering that commands can be locating by quasi-coordinates, you can start to grow comfortable with using the more complex techniques of Word 2010. Each command can be found in a *ribbon* associated with a particular *tab*. Within each tab's ribbon, there are *groups*. Some commands are accessed via the **Launcher** command.

Throughout this book, we have encouraged you to explore the commands and options that *Word* provides. We believe that is by playing with *Word*, you'll get to know it better, and indeed become proficient at using it.

Remember to use *Word Help* if you get stuck. Or try starting over with a new document. By practicing, that is, by using *Word* frequently, you'll get to try new commands and find the ones you need to get your document the way you want it.

Good luck and best wishes. We enjoy using *Word 2010,* and we hope you'll come to enjoy it, too.

Index

LaVergne, TN USA
08 September 2010

196349LV00005B/118/P